Rescued

from

ISIS

Rescued

from

ISIS

The Gripping True Story

of How a Father Saved His Son

Dimitri Bontinck

ST. MARTIN'S PRESS 〠 NEW YORK

Names and identifying details of some of the people portrayed in this book have been changed.

www.stmartins.com

Designed by Steven Seighman

The Library of Congress Cataloging-in-Publication Data is available upon request.

ISBN 978-1-250-14758-5 (hardcover)
ISBN 978-1-250-14759-2 (ebook)

Our books may be purchased in bulk for promotional, educational, or business use. Please contact your local bookseller or the Macmillan Corporate and Premium Sales Department at 1-800-221-7945, extension 5442, or by e-mail at MacmillanSpecialMarkets@macmillan.com.

First Edition: August 2017

10 9 8 7 6 5 4 3 2 1

To my son, with faith in the love that conquers all,
and hope for peace in the world

Rescued

from

ISIS

Prologue: The Basement

DAY AFTER DAY, I kept hearing the words "Kafr Hamra." The Syrian fighters I met told me I had to go to this village with the strange name north of the city I was staying in. *Kafr Hamra. Kafr Hamra.* All the Europeans were there. British, French, Belgian. *Kafr Hamra. It's the base of the Westerners.*

It was like a refrain from a song I couldn't get out of my head no matter how hard I tried. "Have you gone to Kafr Hamra?" people asked, their expressions touched with confusion. Like, what the hell are you doing here in Aleppo? Go to Kafr Hamra. Obviously.

But there was a problem. My driver and many other people were telling me to stay far away from Kafr Hamra. Activists, journalists, ordinary people, and other jihadis were all very firm on this point. The fighters who occupied the village were paranoid, they said, violent, unpredictable. They wouldn't react well to a Westerner just showing up. So what if I was looking for my son? These guys didn't care about that. Exactly what the people of the village would do if a strange pale-faced man knocked on their door wasn't really spelled out, but it was clearly not good.

Everyone agreed that there were European fighters in Kafr Hamra. That wasn't the question. The question was, will you get out of the place with your spleen and your face intact?

So I put off going there. Better to chase down the other leads first. I filed Kafr Hamra under "Last Resorts."

At that moment, I'd been in Syria for two weeks looking for my son. When I'd crossed the border, I'd felt a completely unexpected burst of courage that had carried me through the often chaotic and confusing days ahead. It was like a shot of adrenaline. In fact, before I'd boarded the plane, I'd been thinking I was going to feel the opposite emotion in Syria: total, paralyzing fear. Like when you wonder what you would do in battle, save your buddies or run. That kind of fear.

But no. I felt ten feet tall when I got to Syria—younger, more audacious, ready to take on risks I would have considered nuts back in Belgium. It was a gift. After months of agonizing about what to do about Jay, I was actually on the ground following his trail. I was making contacts. I was getting information; some of it worthless, sure, but some of it leading me closer to my son. I was putting my life on the line, just like his was.

Was I afraid? Yes, sometimes. Very afraid. My hands shook when I lit the shitty bootleg Marlboros that are everywhere in Syria. (Jesus, I would have sold my soul for some real Virginia tobacco.) But honestly, I hadn't felt this alive in years. Believe journalists when they tell you that going to war zones is addictive. I was feeling the first kick of the drug and it was strong.

But those two words, "Kafr Hamra," kept hammering away in the back of my mind. As daring as I felt, I didn't want to go there. I believed the jihadis who told me to avoid it. Some of these men had scars, bullet wounds that hadn't healed properly. They'd seen battle, they'd lost friends, they'd faced tanks and RPGs and Syrian President Bashar al-Assad's planes. Very serious stuff that made them serious people, in my eyes. If they told me to definitely, positively, 100 percent not do something, I was going to listen.

So I didn't go. There's brave, I told myself, and then there's stupid.

After a week more, however, I hadn't found a single other lead on Jay's whereabouts, nothing that any two people on the ground could agree on. I couldn't ignore Kafr Hamra anymore: all signs pointed toward the village. I had to face my fears, or else what was I doing here in Syria but running around like a lunatic and giving the snipers a pale white face to target in their rifle sights?

Either I went to Kafr Hamra or I went home.

I told my driver and the two journalists, Narciso and Joanie, I was traveling with what I'd decided. We drove through Aleppo to the village, passing several checkpoints manned by jihadis on the way. My gut tightened every time a fighter leaned into the window of the car and asked who we were. I said nothing, as

I'd been instructed. Narciso and Joanie also stayed silent. These were the moments we dreaded the most.

I was bone-tired; my skin was peeling from sunburn and I'd already lost ten pounds. If I never saw another plate of hummus again, it would be too soon for me. I wanted a hot shower, a glass of good whiskey, and a real bed. But I couldn't leave Syria without coming to this place.

We pulled up to the villa, larger than I imagined and painted the color of sand. There were two armed men standing guard, their faces covered by balaclavas. They pointed their AK-47s at the hood of the car.

"Who are you?" one said in Arabic.

The driver answered. "He is the father of the Belgian, looking for his son."

The two men consulted between themselves. One of them ran inside. I waited in the car, needing a smoke. Was Jay inside there? Would I see his face and embrace him at last? Or would they tell me that he was dead?

The young man came out of the house. "Only you," he said, pointing to me. "And you two." The Syrians who'd helped me find the place. Narciso and Joanie didn't protest. I got the impression that they were happy to wait outside.

I took a deep breath, opened the car door, and followed the young man. My heart was thumping. There was a row of shoes next to the door to the house. I looked quickly to see if I recognized Jay's, but I didn't want to be seen inspecting the boots and sneakers like a third-rate detective, so I slipped mine off and put them at the end of the row.

My guides stayed in the lobby as I walked inside the villa. The entry opened up into a large living room where sofas were pushed against the wall. There were PlayStation controllers hooked up to a console, their black wires snaking toward a flat-screen TV on the wall. There were dozens of young men here, some of them wearing balaclavas, some not. Their eyes followed me. The room was quiet.

There was a man sitting on a small sofa, alone. He had intense black eyes, a broad nose, long flowing black hair, and a thick black beard. He looked liked Jesus, honestly, which was a bit weird, but then again, so many of the Islamic fighters did. His right leg was pulled up onto the sofa, a cushion beneath the knee. He appeared to be wounded. I didn't find out until later, but this was Abu Absi, the first emir in Syria to swear allegiance to ISIS, something that had happened only months before.

That's what the people in Aleppo had been warning me about. How insane this new group that called itself the "Islamic State" really was. The group didn't use that title, not yet. But they sensed these people were different.

Absi's hand rose and he motioned for me to approach. I took a few steps. I felt that if I moved too suddenly toward the emir—I assumed he was the emir—that I would be cut down by a spray of bullets before I could reach him.

I sat down on the carpet in front of Absi. Before I could begin my appeal, he spoke. "I have no Belgians in my group."

My heart sank. I thought I'd come to the place where I would find Jay. But this statement left me no opening.

"Have you heard . . ." I began.

Absi snapped his fingers. Suddenly, everything in front of me went black as someone yanked a hood over my head. I felt my breath curl back on the skin of my face. A surge of panic shot through my nerves. I yelled out.

Strong hands yanked me to my feet. I was rushed headlong away from the emir. There was shouting behind me. What were they saying?

It was happening, the scenario I'd dreaded. What had happened to Daniel Pearl and other Westerners. Kidnapping, imprisonment, beheading. I tried to get away, but the hands that held my arms were clasped on them with a powerful grip.

I felt the ground beneath my feet fall away. I lurched forward, thinking I was being thrown into a pit. I turned my head away and braced for the impact. But my feet struck something. Stairs. We were going down into the basement.

I clambered down five or six stairs. People were yelling things in Arabic, angry voices. We stopped. The air in the hood was growing hot. I breathed in and out fast.

"What are you doing?" I shouted.

The jihadists began pawing through my pockets. They found my phone and my passport. They took them from me, then stripped off my clothes. Sweat-stained shirt, pants, socks. Something slammed into my ribs. A fist, I thought. The pain radiated through my torso and I curled over.

"How did you know where we were?" a voice yelled in English. "Who gave you our location?"

I couldn't breathe. I wheezed out a few words.

"A . . . a fighter told me."

"Which fighter? Who?"

"I don't know his name. In Aleppo. He was in Aleppo."

I really didn't know his name. There had been more than one.

"Is your son giving you information about our group? Tell us!"

I froze. Did that mean my son was here? And now they thought he was a spy? If so, that was very bad.

"No, never!" I yelled. "I found this place on my own."

Something—the butt of a rifle, I think—slammed into the side of my head. Streaks of white exploded behind my eyes and tumbled in all directions. I sank to the ground, my head falling forward.

Don't be afraid, I whispered to myself. *Everyone has a father. Everyone recognizes the love of a parent for his child. This is universal.*

Through the cloth, I could see a bright light shining just a few feet from my eyes. It seemed to follow me, a halo in the blackness. *They're filming this,* I thought to myself. Just like Danny Pearl. I had a quick flash of how I would look in the video: a crouching half-naked figure in a black hood. *One of them is holding a knife right now, one of the men gathered around me. He is waiting for his moment. A signal.*

This is how it ends, I thought. I'm going to die without ever seeing my son again.

Chapter One

WHAT LED ME TO SYRIA in 2013 to rescue my only son from the grips of ISIS? It was genetics and geography and a Moroccan girl and a small crack that opened in my son's mind after a breakup. But I must trace part of the story back to my own beginnings.

I was born in Flanders, which is the Dutch-speaking part of Belgium, and raised a Catholic. My family was a mix of liberals and devout Christians. I can remember going to my uncle's house and picking up his copy of a newspaper that arrived with strange foreign postmarks. I would read out the name of the paper: "*PRAVDA*," with its odd typography. (The crossing line in the A's always had two bars. So cool-looking!) My uncle believed the Revolution was just around the corner, and the world would soon be a better place.

He read his *PRAVDA* and went to May Day rallies. My other relatives went to church and prayed for the souls of the lost and worked hard and volunteered when they could. I got from both sides of my family a belief that, whatever path I chose in life, I should help to change things for the better. This was reinforced in Catholic school, which I attended for years.

I've always been an idealist. I was always looking for a cause to believe in. I wanted someone to show me the true way to save the planet, or at least a few of the people on it.

I was impatient to begin my life. When I was seventeen, I dropped out of high school and volunteered for the "land forces," which is what we called the Belgian Army. I was placed in an infantry battalion. To me, being a soldier meant helping people. It seemed like a simple idea.

There was a second reason I joined the Army: American war movies. I absolutely loved them, and that drove me to want to be a soldier: *Platoon. The Deer Hunter. Apocalypse Now.* Those movies were so alive that you would walk out of the theater buzzing with electricity, your skin tingling. What would it be like to be in a shooting war? How would I perform? Most young men want to be heroes, to rescue someone from some terrible fate. I felt this, too, deeply.

It never occurred to me that those movies always seemed to end badly. I was nineteen. I didn't care about endings.

At the time I joined the Belgian military, the Yugoslav wars were ongoing, and I was assigned to a United Nations peacekeeping unit, as part of the Belgian commitment to the UN. I traded in my green helmet for a blue one and my buddies and I became "observers" to the simmering war zone. I was as excited as hell.

We were sent to Slovenia to keep the peace between the warring factions. Slovenia had declared its independence from Yugoslavia on June 25, 1991, and a short, violent war between the Yugoslav Army and the Slovenian rebels quickly followed. A peace treaty was signed, but the hatred and resentment didn't go away. We were there to make sure people stopped killing each other over these ancient feuds. As observers, we weren't supposed to get involved in any real action. We were spectators with guns. But there was violence all around us.

One time we were driving down a street in a small white armored vehicle with UN painted on the side in tall black letters. The sound of the huge rubber tires made a steady humming noise on the asphalt. It was a warm, beautiful day, with blue skies visible through the hatch above.

We came to a roadblock. Through the small spy-hole in the front of the tank, we could see armed men approaching. And then, suddenly, the snout of a rifle was stuffed through the spy-hole.

Time stopped. I stared at the worn black steel of the rifle barrel. This wasn't a film. Francis Ford Coppola wasn't behind me with a camera, telling me how to act. The Kalashnikov was ten inches from my face, and there were real bullets in the magazine. I could barely catch my breath.

Adrenaline made me want to grab the rifle and shove it out of the way. But it was no time for heroics. Our captain called out that we were contacting headquarters and that, if they pulled the trigger, there would be an international incident. We called headquarters. And watched the rifle snout. And tried not to move suddenly.

After ten minutes, the Kalashnikov was withdrawn, but the armed men still stood in our way in the road. Our commanders negotiated with their commanders; we sat in the vehicle as the evening grew cold. Finally, some kind of agreement was reached and we were allowed to drive on.

A first taste of aggression. It had been interesting, but I'll never forget that cold, metallic feeling in my gut that told me something awful was just seconds away from happening.

Two months later, we were in our fortified observation post, looking out at a border town. There were sandbags stacked on top of each other to block any bullets from getting through, and a boom box playing rock, loudly. Someone had popped in the cassette of a Stones record, *Aftermath*. We were bored out of our skulls. Our jokes were getting old; all our stories of getting in trouble in school or getting lucky with this or that girl had been told three or four times.

All of a sudden, gunfire erupted a hundred yards away. We could see the tracers. Coming toward us.

For some reason, my first memory of that moment is what was playing in the background. "Paint It Black." *Dun-dun-dun-dun-dun-dun*, Keith Richard's evil guitar licks with Charlie Watts pounding out a sinister rhythm on the drums. It was so surreal, so *right*. We seemed to have entered a war film. We began laughing like jackals and yelling to each other that this was just like *Apocalypse Now*. Just like it!

We weren't allowed to fire back, as our lives weren't in real danger, at least until the guys shooting at us improved their aim. We couldn't tell where the fire was coming from anyway. But the experience of being fired on was exhilarating. It felt like we'd been baptized. Welcome to war.

I never shot anyone. I never even fired my gun. But I saw people shooting and being shot and it injected a bit of antifreeze into my veins. That would become important later. Not that I'd been really tested in a war zone, not yet. But you need to hear bullets and get used to having guns pointed at you to go to places like Syria.

When I got leave from the Army, I decided to go to West Africa on vacation. I always loved to travel to distant places, something I'd never had a chance to do as a boy with my family. Slovenia had been fun, but I wanted to go somewhere unlike any place I'd ever visited.

In Africa, I found everything fresh and different. The sounds, the tastes, the view of life. In the small villages in a place like Nigeria, you can hear the monkeys in the jungle shaking the branches as they race through the trees. The smell of dust in the air, the women squatting by the side of the road bartering their goods, that special African kind of scene that can't be duplicated anywhere else. I was entranced.

In the second week of my vacation, I met a local named Helen, a Nigerian girl with a gorgeous smile. She looked innocent, like a baby, with her big brown eyes and girlish figure. Later, I found out that inside she was tough, a fighter, but in the beginning I felt like protecting her. Our eyes locked and we began talking. Talking led to other things and, within a couple months after meeting, Helen was pregnant.

Interracial relationships aren't that common in Belgium. When I brought her home to Flanders, I got looks on the street, no question. But racism was foreign to me. I didn't care. I loved Helen and wanted to be with her and our child.

Helen wanted to get married in Nigeria in her home village. I jumped at the chance. Helen's father was an important person in Benin City in Southern Nigeria, a leader of a prominent tribe. Her family wanted a traditional marriage. I agreed—who wants a boring Dutch wedding? My marriage seemed to be sealed in adventure—not only the romance of love, but the romance of new sensations, new places.

I spent many happy hours in the village, talking with Helen's uncles and cousins. I wanted to know everything: How had their ancestors lived? Did their traditional medicine—the herbs and the roots that the medicine men gave the sick—really work, or was it all psychological? They taught me about voodoo, and I watched as holy men sacrificed goats and chickens, dancing and spraying the animals' blood in wide red arcs as they performed their ceremonies. They handed me animal skulls that were filled with water and told me to drink.

During our wedding, I was dressed in a traditional African long shirt and Helen was resplendent in a bright native dress. We returned to Belgium after the wedding and there, on January 29, 1995, Jejoen was born. I immediately nicknamed him "Jay." It was a moment of great harmony for me. I was thrilled to have a son. Here was someone to play football with, to go waterskiing with, to talk about girls when he became interested in them.

He was a dream boy.

Chapter Two

SINCE HELEN WAS A CATHOLIC, we decided to raise Jay the same way, although I'd lost my faith years before. But the strict education he received in Antwerp, the city we lived in, wasn't needed to keep him in line. Jay was a joy to be with. He never gave us any trouble. He was an easy child, a natural athlete with a pleasant, open smile. When his little sister was born, Jay became a loving big brother.

I have so many memories of his childhood. He was a fanatic for a few songs, which he demanded we play over and over whenever we were in the car. His favorite of all was "Angelina" by Harry Belafonte. "Play it, Daddy!" he would cry. He could be a bit headstrong, and wouldn't stop calling out to me until the first notes began. *Angelina, Angelina, please bring down your concertina.* I would look in the rearview mirror and find him lisping along to the lyrics. As for movies, Walt Disney's *Pinocchio* was the one. Every time we watched it together, snuggled up on our couch, he would sit silently and follow the puppet's story, completely absorbed. And then, every time, when it ended, he would cry. He would never tell me why this was, but I think he loved Pinocchio so much that he hated to leave him.

He wasn't like every other boy. At six years old, Jay had a collection of dinosaurs and could name each one: raptor, T. rex, brontosaurus. Every other boy I've seen with these toys would end up having them fight each other. Could the raptor beat the Saurischia, the lizard-hipped dinosaur? Who was the strongest of them all?

But not Jay. He wanted all his dinosaurs, even the raptors, to live in peace and harmony. When I came upon him playing with the toys, they would all be arranged in a line going on some adventure, or they would be climbing onto the couch, the bigger beasts helping the smaller one. There was never any battle. He was gentle in his heart.

If there was any inkling of the future, it came with Jay's restlessness. He was always seeking. He took up kickboxing and diving; he got an international license in windsurfing. We did board surfing together. He was a break-dancer, so good that as a teenager he was chosen to appear on a TV show called *Move Like Michael Jackson*. Out of six thousand candidates, ninety-five were chosen to compete and Jay was one of them. He didn't make the finals, but he impressed everyone, especially the host.

Jay was always looking at the horizon, wondering what was next in his life. He reminded me of me, honestly. We were close, two dreamers in a difficult, exciting world. We'd go to Burger King, one of his favorite places, and talk about his life and plans.

We had our fights, too, but they were small ones. I was a

liberal father. When he wanted to smoke, I said, "Try it." Better he talks to me about these things than runs off to do them in secret.

Jay grew up as a completely ordinary Belgian boy. He drank once in a while; he played the guitar, like I did. We would plug in our axes and jam together. "Can you please keep it down?" Helen would yell from the next room, and we would cackle and dive into the next riff. He went to clubs. He had friends of all different colors and faiths.

Jay was curious, like a sponge. At fourteen years old, I found him reading books about the Freemasons, and then about the Knights Templar. These young men who'd tried to change the world just fascinated him. In the town of Bruges, not too far from where we lived, there is a twelfth-century church called the Basilica of the Holy Blood that's said to hold a phial of Christ's blood, brought back to Belgium after the Second Crusade. The phial is carried out of the church once every year during a famous procession that threads through Bruges's streets. Jay grew up hearing about such things, in a country where faith and heroics often mixed.

I was proud of the life we were giving Jay and his sister. Growing up, my family hadn't been able to afford guitars and trips to Italy and America. When you're a father, you want your son to have what was always out of your reach as a boy. And Jay had it.

We wanted him to feel connected to his African heritage, too, so my wife often brought him to Nigeria. He got to meet his relatives, to see the places where his family came from, to spend time with his cousins. We thought we were doing everything right, grounding him in his past. We knew that being a biracial boy in Belgium wasn't the same thing as being blue-eyed and blond-haired. But perhaps we opened up a gap between his two worlds that he found hard to cross.

I thought he would become a lawyer or a politician, while he was looking forward to a career as a pilot. Like me, he wanted to travel and see the places that others shied away from. *Fine,* I thought. When I retire, I told Jay, I'll go with you to Belize and Vancouver and Rio de Janeiro. That was the dream.

Perhaps I didn't understand what it's like to be a mixed-race child in Belgium. I'd never had to choose between two cultures, to wonder who I was and where I belonged. By the time Jay was fifteen, there were little signs of strain in his life. He didn't pass his exams that year and had to change schools. He left Our Lady College, the Jesuit institution that he loved, and transferred to a remedial school. At the same time, he and his girlfriend of three years, a blond Belgian girl from a Christian home, broke up.

It was a double blow. After the split, Jay stayed in his room for hours at a time. He didn't want to talk about what had happened. When you look at such breakups as a parent, you think it's a minor blip in an otherwise wonderful life. But for a teenager, it's disaster. He was in the abyss, and for a young kid, there seems to be no way out.

Jay found a new girlfriend, a Muslim Moroccan girl. When they first started talking, she asked him, "Why don't you convert to Islam?" I'm sure her heart was in the right place—she liked Jay and wanted good things for him, and to her that meant spiritual enlightenment through Islam. But that tiny little phrase, dropped into the life of a boy who was searching, hit like a grenade.

My son went on the computer and typed in the words "What is Islam?" He knew nothing about the faith, really—nothing positive, nothing negative. He just wanted to talk to a girl. He found the Islam entry on Wikipedia and began to read.

Thirty seconds. That's all it takes to change your life.

Jay had my adventurous genes, my thirst to find answers to the big questions in life. He'd broken up with a girl, and he wanted to remake himself. It could have been something else he fell into—professional kickboxing, Zen Buddhism, meditation—but it just happened that the Moroccan girl placed a certain word in his head. And it sprouted like a seed.

But still, just a seed! There are millions of people around the world who discover Islam and live happy, peaceful lives. Our son wasn't lost yet. He was looking for tranquility, inner peace, a way to serve. What he found was very different.

I didn't know much about Islam. I had a slightly negative view of it, from reading about the unrest and violence in Islamic countries. It seemed to me that people in those nations couldn't live in peace. Why was that? Did it have anything to do with their faith? Honestly, I had no idea. It wasn't a major priority in my life, learning about the schism between Sunni and Shiite or whatever. I was working in the police court, which is part of the Belgian justice system, trying to earn a living for my family. I was oblivious.

After a while, Internet searches no longer satisfied Jay, so he went looking for real flesh-and-blood Muslims. He went to a small mosque called De-Koepel in the Borgerhout neighborhood. The imam there was Sulayman Van Ael, who was himself a convert and who practiced and preached a moderate form of Islam. The two met and Jay told the imam how he'd discovered this new faith within himself. He wanted to convert and to start a new life.

Though my son was only sixteen, the imam complied. Any male past the age of puberty is allowed to convert.

I wonder where I was that moment on August 1, 2011, the moment my son stood up in the mosque, a microphone in his hand and prepared to embark on a new life. Was I shopping for groceries or watching a soccer game? Was I just then picking up the remote to switch to another program? Half a mile from my house, unknown to me, my son changed. He bent down to the microphone and said these words, *"La ilaha illa Allah, Muhammad rasoolu Allah." There is no true god but Allah, and I bear witness that Muhammad is His Messenger.*

Maybe I clicked the remote from channel two to channel four. Or I picked up a box of cereal and looked at the sugar content. And in that moment, it was done.

The condo we lived in wasn't too far from the neighborhood called De Coninckplein. That particular place had many North African immigrants, many of whom were Muslim, a small percentage of whom had become radicalized. This was the second piece in the puzzle of my son's story: geography. It just so happened we lived near a hotbed of jihadis.

Jay's friend Azzedine lived in that neighborhood, and just about two hundred yards from his family's place was a nondescript house located at 117 Dambruggestraat. It was the headquarters of a group called Sharia4Belgium. They were radical Salafists, the most extreme branch of Islam. The organization's members demanded that Belgium become an Islamic state, ruled by sharia law. The prime minister would be replaced by a caliph, the parliament would become a shura council, and all non-Muslims would be forced either to leave the country or to pay the *jizya,* a tax on all unbelievers.

What an outrageous idea! Only 6 percent of the country's people were Muslim, and that population was mixed between many different faiths: Sunni, Shia, Ahmadi, and others. But the idea was meant to provoke. To draw a line between believers and nonbelievers.

I didn't know much about Sharia4Belgium. Like many people in my country, I found them to be extremists, but they had nothing to do with my life. I would see one of the members on the evening news every so often, usually the group's short, vigorous spokesman, Fouad Belkacem. He would make some controversial statement and I would roll my eyes. Once he said that he prayed for Osama bin Laden; another time he declared that gay people should be put to death.

Hateful nonsense. But he was a guy on television. I mostly ignored him.

In the winter of 2011, Azzedine invited Jay to a meeting at

the headquarters, which were really just a series of rented rooms. Jay said no. His mosque considered the men of Sharia4Belgium to be extremists. Jay was still learning what the religion was, and in the opinion of his new friends, the brothers of this fringe group were bomb-throwers. They hurt Islam with their ridiculous statements. So Jay turned down the invitation.

But Jay was still a teenager, and teenagers change their mind. A week or so later, Azzedine asked again and Jay didn't want to be rude by turning down a second invite. What did he have to lose? One Sunday, he agreed to go. Not because he was looking to become a jihadi, but because he was curious and wanted to be a good friend.

At the mosque, Jay met Fouad Belkacem. The thirty-three-year-old spokesman had been born in a small town between Antwerp and Brussels to Moroccan parents. He'd fallen into the criminal lifestyle and become a forger and a member of a large drug-smuggling ring. He was a former thief who'd been arrested for burglary three times. When Belkacem wasn't in prison, he sometimes worked at a youth center, where he told the kids that gays were vermin and that democracy was doomed.

Belkacem was young and energetic, with a round face, a shaven head, a mustache, and a thick black beard. He wore rimless glasses and often had a white prayer shawl over his head. And he was charismatic. Even I have to admit this. He was cocky and confident and the energy just seemed to pour off him. "We simply can not lose" was one of his favorite quotes. He meant that Belgium would one day become part of the global Islamic caliphate.

To Jay, Belkacem was a revelation. He had a way of talking that was both street-smart and filled with historical anecdotes and knowledge. My son would later say it was like being injected with a drug. The fog of Jay's life parted and he saw the world clearly for the first time in many months. The chaos of his existence, his search for a way to lead a meaningful life, was whisked away.

But my son was still loyal to Van Ael, the imam at his mosque. Belkacem sneered when the name came up. He wrote up a list of questions for Van Ael, and told Jay to deliver them. They would soon find out who was preaching the true faith.

One of the questions was about whether or not hatred of others was part of Islam. Van Ael told my son it wasn't, and that Belkacem was peddling a distorted version of the Koran that would lead Jay into danger. Jay trudged back to the Sharia4Belgium headquarters and repeated the answer to Belkacem. The imam's eyes lit up. He pulled out his Koran and began reading passages that advocated hatred of other faiths. One after the other.

It had been a test—a trick, really. And Belkacem won.

The radical preacher was the final piece of the puzzle for Jay. Belkacem told Jay that he was joining a movement that would soon sweep across the world, that he was doing God's work. My son's existence—friends, soccer, rap, dancing—now seemed laughably small to him. Here was an epic life waiting for him, a way to rebel and live forever as a martyr. What teenager could resist?

Chapter Three

THE FIRST SIGN I SAW of Jay's new faith was the cap he wore, the round kufi. I was startled by it—*What the hell is he wearing on his head?* I asked him about it and we got into a little bit of an argument. I do have a temper, I have to admit. But it wasn't that big a deal.

I assumed the cap was a fad, a phase Jay was going through. He would get tired of it and be back to the baseball caps he loved so much. Last year, it had been Converse All Stars, this year it's a Muslim cap. Fine. I was shocked to think that he was getting interested in Islam, but the way he explained it to me, I could see its appeal. He talked about the mystical core of the faith, the myths and the stories. And the brotherhood with millions of other Muslims around the world.

Things snowballed. I began seeing Jay around Antwerp with his new friends, all of them wearing the Islamic dress and the kufi. His old pals, the blond girls and blue-eyed boys, disappeared. He gave up dancing, which I knew he loved; he put away his guitar, quit his sports teams. He told my wife and me that he would only accept halal food from now on and began eating on his own, in his room or at restaurants with his friends. I'd always loved to have dinner with my family, but now there was an empty chair where Jay used to sit.

I didn't know it then, but Jay was slowly burying his old life. He only wore white now, like a newborn, and that was the point. The son I knew was dead and in his place had arrived a Muslim child. They'd even given him a new name, "Sayfullah." The first time I heard it, I was confused. Who was Sayfullah? I went to the Internet and typed it into Google. Sayfullah, it turns out, means "the sword of Allah." It was the name given to one of Muhammad's original companions, a warrior so fierce that he'd broken nine swords in one battle with the Roman army.

This was the name they had chosen for my gentle-hearted son, in secret. One marked by blood and violence. I felt chills.

The brothers also gave Jay a *kunya,* or nickname, which is common for budding radicals who want to disguise their true identity. Jay's was "Abu Assya." But it was more than a change in friends and a new name. Something in my son's face had altered. The softness was gone. He looked at my wife and me differently now. Cold. Hard. As if we were strangers he'd bumped into at a railway station.

His new faith started causing friction at home. Jay got home late now after sessions at Sharia4Belgium that ran into the small hours of the morning. He neglected his studies; his grades sank down to near-failing. He didn't have time to read about history or chemistry; he was consumed with the Koran. His Catholic education, which we'd invested so much in, was blown away like scattered wheat.

His friends from the radical sect never came to our house. They'd done this many times before; they had a plan, and part of it was not to create any scenes at the believer's home. It was a stealth operation from the beginning, and they had years of experience in such things.

That New Year's Eve, my aunts and uncles came to visit our house in Antwerp. The holiday was special to me and my family. We saw relatives we didn't get to see for most of the year; we drank brandy and ate delicious cakes. We gossiped, told old stories, and a few lies. It was a way to reconnect with the people we loved, the people we'd come from. And the children always greeted their relatives at the door, welcoming them to our house with a handshake and a kiss.

When my aunts and uncles came through the doorway that year, Jay in his kufi shook the hands of the men. But when his aunts, their eyes sparkling, extended their hands, my son put his own behind his back.

I saw this happen and went rigid with shock.

"Jay, what's going on?" I said. Maybe I shouted it, I don't know.

Jay wouldn't say anything. His jawline was set. And he had this look of contempt in his eyes. But whatever we said, his two hands remained behind his back.

I was pissed off. How dare he disrespect his own family, the women who'd held him when he was just an infant and loved him from then on? What was he thinking? It was as if he was erasing all those years of love and family reunions, throwing them away. His aunts, confused, looked at him with hurt eyes. Furious, I yelled at him to go to his room. He sulked, then obeyed.

My son continued to change before my eyes. He stopped listening to music, going out to movies. Instead, I came home to find my son praying or on the Internet. He began to grow his beard.

I didn't know it then, but Jay had started on a twenty-four-week course in ideology at Sharia4Belgium. Belkacem began teaching my son his own hard-line view of Islam. Everything was black and white: One was either a Muslim or an infidel. One either followed sharia or democracy. One either followed the path of jihad or one was an imposter.

There was more, of course: Women were subservient to men, and men could take multiple wives. Jews and gay people were dirt. Sharia courts administered the only true justice in the land. The earth belonged to the Muslims, who'd been defrauded of their rightful inheritance by the crusading infidels and the scheming Jews, but their time was coming. The new worldwide caliphate would be ushered in through bloodshed.

There was no air in this "pure" Islam, no mercy, no room for harmony. Only division and hatred.

Belkacem reinforced this hard-line view with physical training. Jay was an accomplished kickboxer, but now he took a full martial arts class. Sharia4Belgium was toughening his body right along with his soul. He watched videos of radical preachers from the Middle East and London, and DVDs that showed actual battles from Afghanistan. As a teenager, I'd fallen in love with *Apocalypse Now* and *Platoon,* but Jay was being fed the real thing. He even watched videos of beheadings.

The group was normalizing violence. Normalizing jihad. It was in the air Jay breathed.

What did he find in Islam that he didn't find in his life in the West? Order and discipline, I think. Life is complicated, especially for a teenager, and the faith provided him a map through even the smallest difficulties. He was a seeker for the truth, and here was someone telling him, "Look no further. We are the real thing."

I think now that my son had no role models, not good ones, anyway. I grew up with JFK and Martin Luther King, Jr. Who does Jay's generation have? Justin Bieber? Lady Gaga? There was something missing in the culture that we've produced in the last few decades, I think, that prepared the way for people like Jay to seek a better way elsewhere.

At the headquarters of Sharia4Belgium, Jay was following a strict regimen. He'd start with an hour lecture where Belkacem spun another web of fantasies about the supremacy of Islam. Then he'd shuttle to another room where instructors led the young men in combat training, wrestling, and calisthenics. We'd be at home, sitting on the couch and talking about normal things, when he'd get texts summoning him to 117 Dambruggestraat. It was as if he was a soldier who was always ready for a call-up to his unit. I thought my son had discovered a faith, but he was actually being prepped for war.

After a few months of indoctrination, my son was sent out onto the streets. He stood behind Belkacem as he spouted his poison to passersby. Sharia4Belgium even sent him to playgrounds in North African neighborhoods, where he would seek out children and tell them not to neglect their faith and to hate their homeland.

I knew nothing about this at first. Then one evening, Helen and I were sitting on the couch in our condo, watching TV. The evening news came on. One of the first stories was about a Kalashnikov rifle discovered at the headquarters of Sharia4Belgium. Before I could react, the program cut to a video of Fouad Belkacem giving a speech in one of Antwerp's main boulevards, surrounded by his followers. Just to the spokesman's left sat a young man. My eyes darted to this person's face and I felt a sick electric shock pass through my heart. It was Jay.

It was like seeing your son at the left hand of the devil. I panicked. I picked up my cell phone and called the police. "My son is with Sharia4Belgium," I told him. "You have to get him out of there!" I must not have been the first parent to call, because they had their answer ready. *We can't remove your son,* they told me. *There is a thing called freedom of association. If he's there under his own free will, that is his right.*

I refused to accept this. The boy was just sixteen! This wasn't conversion, it was a kind of kidnapping. There must be something they could do! Finally, the authorities sent over a social worker to interview Jay in our condo. They disappeared into his room and I could hear them talking. When she emerged, Jay looked at me almost pityingly. The woman had come to discuss his Islamic radicalization but she didn't even know where Mecca was. It was a total failure.

I knew then that Belgium was asleep. The West was asleep. Radical Islam had come right to the door of my home, stolen inside, and taken my son, and we had no laws, no formulas to stop it. In fact, the Islamists were using the great strength of the West—our freedoms—against us.

What I was slowly learning was that no one wanted to talk about this enormous danger. They *wanted* to be asleep, and dream that the problem would go away. I felt like I was standing at a new Ground Zero, shouting a warning, but that the world had closed its ears.

Day after day, our lives continued down the same sad path. Every day I saw my son, nodded to him in the kitchen. I heard him speaking Arabic on the phone. Who was this boy? Where had he come from? If he looked at us like we were strangers, we could only return the same gaze.

Every week seemed to bring a new low. In February 2012, the principal of the school Jay was attending called the police. Jay had issued a threat: he was going to "purge" the school of its nonbelievers.

Unknown to us, this was a crucial moment. We had two choices as parents: either oppose Jay's newfound interest in Islam or try to understand it. Now, after what I've been through,

I would tell parents: Don't put all the blame on the mosque or the organization that helped convert your son. By doing so, you only increase the glamour of the group in your son's eyes. It's as if he brought home a girlfriend you didn't approve of, one who had a prison record and a neck tattoo. What do you do? If you scream at your son that she is a disaster, he falls more deeply in love. If you invite her over for lunch and play nice, perhaps he calms down and sees her as she really is.

We went with Option A. Because we'd never done this before. Because we panicked. But we were wrong. I should have asked Jay: What did you find in Islam? Why are you so devoted to it? I should have seen the world through his eyes. But instead, I was a typical parent. Arguments filled our small condo and any idea of family harmony fled out onto the street and never came back.

I did make one attempt to understand Sharia4Belgium. I called Fouad Belkacem and invited him to my house. I had to meet this man and try to comprehend why Jay saw so much in him. Belkacem immediately agreed to come. It wasn't what I expected; I thought he would be evasive or hostile. Instead, he was almost eager to meet me.

He arrived one afternoon trailed by his followers. I ushered them all into my living room. They sat down, Belkacem in his flowing djellaba, the long loose-fitting robe that most Islamists wear. He shook my hand, smiled, and began to speak.

Instantly I saw why my son had fallen under his spell. Charisma is palpable and Belkacem had it.

He denied everything, of course. Training my son to do jihad? *Shocking, I'll look into it.* Jay's rebellious attitude? *Unac-*

ceptable for a Muslim child. He shot Jay a warning look. "He needs to be home in the evening. Mr. Bontinck"—it was always "Mr. Bontinck"—"I'll make sure Jay does the right thing." He told me the organization was misunderstood. They had nothing to hide. They were doing charity and outreach to suffering people. "You can come see our headquarters if you like. Look around! It will make you feel better." This was part of their strategy: Real information about the group was never to be shared with the families of the believers. The radical literature that they used was stored in the homes of the members, not at the headquarters. It was like the KGB, but for jihadis.

They even spoke to my wife. "Normally, we don't talk to women," Belkacem said, "but in this case . . ." And he smiled. Unconsciously, I was a little grateful to him for making this exception. Now I realize what excellent salesmen they were. They refused all offers of coffee and food, but in every other way they were gracious and seemingly open-minded.

If I had been sixteen, I might have fallen for Belkacem's charm, too. But there was something about the body language of his followers that spooked me. They only spoke when their leader indicated they should. They were hiding something, I could just feel it.

I took up Belkacem on his offer. I started going to the headquarters, walking in around 8:00 P.M. when the lectures began. I thought to myself, *I'll catch them doing something illegal, the authorities will arrest Belkacem and shut the place down. Bingo.* From the outside, the headquarters looked like a normal brick house. Inside, when you entered, there was a normal living room with a TV and sofas along the walls. In back, there was a prayer and lecture room. The kitchen was to the left. It was just an ordinary Belgian home; I'd been in dozens like it during my life. It was as if Sharia4Belgium was saying, *We're as boring as an Antwerp clock-making shop. Come in and have a look around, you'll find nothing to upset you.*

The house was always crowded with believers, young men in djellabas. They would look at me and some even greeted me, nodding and smiling. But that feeling of a secret I was not being told about persisted. What I was seeing was not the real operation, not the real point of Sharia4Belgium.

I sat and listened to the lectures. One night, it would be about Afghanistan and the fate of the Taliban. The next would be about Syria, the third night about racism and Islamophobia. The speakers insisted that Muslims were being targeted worldwide and that their fellow believers must go to their side to help them. Christians were corrupt and greedy; they wanted Muslim lands for their own enrichment.

The speakers were forceful, but they never mentioned the dreaded words: "Jihad." "Warfare." "Guns." The group knew that the government was watching them. So they were being careful.

Still, you could feel the rage in the room. The voices of the speakers were impassioned, sometimes infuriated. *Look what the unbeliever is doing to our brothers and sisters!* was the message. And I could tell it was hitting home.

What struck me especially was that everyone in the rooms except Belkacem and a few of his lieutenants were young. There were no graybeards here. Sharia4Belgium was obviously targeting teenagers and those in their early twenties. Why? Because they are searching and they are naive.

The second time I went to the headquarters, I saw Jay. He was in the back room and he was not happy to see me. I was a ridiculous version of the parent who strolls into to the teenage party and embarrasses his children by watching to see if anyone drinks tequila or smokes a doobie. I never wanted to be that guy, because that guy is an asshole. But here I was. The stakes were too high for me to sit at home and twiddle my thumbs. "I'm just studying my Arabic," he said when I asked what he was learning at the house. "OK," I said. And I kept going back.

One day, I brought a friend of mine, a Muslim my age who'd grown up in Iran. He sat with me and listened to the speeches while his eyes roamed around the sofas and the floor. It was the same speech that night that I'd already heard a couple of times: we Muslims are in a clash of civilizations and Islam is being destroyed before our very eyes. I found it somewhat boring by now. Couldn't these kids see that Muslims were flourishing in the West, living free prosperous lives? It was their own governments that were repressing them and snuffing the life out of them. But here, the West was the villain, always.

Afterward, I asked my friend what he thought. He gave me a troubled look. "Be careful, Dimitri," he said. "Many of these kids will end up in war zones as jihadis. They are turning them into fighters." I was . . . well, I was shocked. My son saw something in that house. I saw a second reality. Now my friend was seeing battlefields. What was real and what was just panic?

Jay brought his Arabic textbooks home to study, and I got used to seeing them around the house. But one evening, as he slipped into his room, I saw an unfamiliar booklet in his hand. I knocked on his door. "What's this book?" I asked. It was a pamphlet, and on the back I recognized the seal of Saudi Arabia.

But it was in Arabic, and I couldn't read it. I accepted Jay's explanation, which I forget today. Something innocent, something about the faith. I nodded, but I felt like a game was being played, and I was the chump.

The stress notched up another level. I was already smoking two packs of Marlboros a day, up from my usual single pack. I was having trouble sleeping. I had the feeling that, while I rested, invisible robbers were combing through my home, stealing my most valuable possessions. What ran through my head again and again were two questions: Where did I fail as a father? What did we do wrong? It was a waste of time. I should have been looking forward to the next emergency instead of wondering what had caused the last one.

The tension seeped into my marriage. That year, in 2012, Helen and I were divorced. With all the commotion in our home, we just weren't getting along and decided it was best to split. We still lived together in our condo in Antwerp, so nothing changed in our living conditions. Some people would later tell me they believed Jay's radicalization began with my divorce. You can never really know what's going on in a teenager's mind, but I don't believe that's true. Jay certainly wasn't happy about our split, but his frustration with where his life was going and his ever-deepening devotion to Islam had begun months before.

It's not easy being the father of a budding jihadi. There's the chaos at home, where you and your wife and your daughter feel like something has ripped apart your family life. And there's the social angle. When I tried to explain to friends and coworkers what I was going through, they would be sympathetic at first. But when they heard the name "Sharia4Belgium," their faces just froze. They hated the group so much, this group that wanted to destroy the nation we all lived in. They might have a flicker of sympathy for me as a father, but the truth was my son had crossed over and joined the enemy. And that made me suspect as well.

What could I say to them, that he was a good boy before it had all happened? That Belkacem was brainwashing him? They looked at the evening news and saw my son standing guard over a monster and I too became tainted by radicalism. It was like being a leper back in the Middle Ages. I felt like I had a sign hung around my neck. "MY SON IS A JIHADI. UNCLEAN. UNCLEAN."

Jay did good things, too. He went to the homes of Muslims suffering from cancer and other horrible diseases and knelt by their beds and prayed for them. If you were suffering from clinical depression and my son heard about it, he would go and chant some verses for courage and patience. Women began contacting Jay and asking him to come by and pray for them.

This was my son, the Jay I knew. A good-hearted boy. Who liked girls.

But Belkacem took this compassion and twisted it. He and his brothers took Jay to "exorcism" sessions, known as *ruqya*. In Islam, it's believed that malevolent spirits, called jinns, can invade the bodies of believers. When this is brought to the attention of Islamic authorities, sometimes a *ruqya* is ordered. A man wearing white gloves kneels at the head of the possessed person and touches her forehead as he chants verses from the Koran. Some believers beat the person or burn red pepper in the room and roll the possessed one in a carpet.

Later on, I found out that during one such ceremony, a woman died as the brothers tried to extract an evil spirit from her body. Jay saw this. He was chanting as it happened. Even if the intent of the brothers was a good one, they exposed my son to death.

During one *ruqya*, Jay went to the home of a family whose father had just died. The session was to bring healing to the mourning children. There he met the man's daughter and the two began talking. Before long, they considered themselves engaged. Jay was being drawn deeper into this strange world than I ever thought possible.

Chapter Four

BY 2013, 2,500 MILES AWAY from us, the Syrian Civil War was raging. The Free Syrian Army had taken up arms against the Assad regime and the fighting turned savage almost immediately. Women and children were torn apart by bombs and artillery strikes, and in the Internet Age, someone was always there to film the aftermath.

I watched the footage on the news and felt my heart sink. These poor innocent people were being brutalized by forces beyond their control. But it was something that I watched on television. Little did I know I would soon be walking among the ruins and the sniper nests myself.

Up until then, the focus of Sharia4Belgium had been on my country. Now it looked south to the newest war in the Middle East. In his lectures, Belkacem began talking with his acolytes about the videos of brutality and death that were all over the Internet. Jay, too, was watching these videos on Facebook and YouTube. After the lectures at Sharia4Belgium, he and his brothers talked about which country they wanted to wage jihad in. Libya? Syria? Somalia? Going to war was almost an expectation; it was ordinary.

Jay was visibly distressed by the videos. Here were his fellow Muslims suffering. "Depart for jihad in Syria!" the voices on the video said. "Defend your faith!" *Where are the heroes?*, the voices of women cried out, *Where are the soldiers of Islam?* I can imagine Jay watching these scenes hour after hour and growing desperate to help. The brainwashing that he'd undergone with Sharia4Belgium had prepared him for this second wave of propaganda.

The complexities of the Syrian conflict didn't interest him; he just wanted to help those faces he saw on his computer screen, and he wanted to do it now. One group of clerics in Saudi Arabia issued a statement online: "The holy warriors of Syria are defending the whole Islamic nation. Trust them and support them because if they are defeated, God forbid, it will be the turn of one Sunni country after another." So it was as if the elders of the faith had approved this war, and called all good Muslims to it.

In September 2012, a trailer for a film called *Innocence of Muslims* was uploaded on YouTube. It was a fourteen-minute video written by an Egyptian and it depicted the mistreatment of Christians in that country, along with the rising oppression practiced by the government. Then it went on to some really controversial things: it portrayed Muhammad as a child molester, a fool, a homosexual, and a brutal criminal. Jay and his brothers were outraged and took to the streets to protest the film.

His anger burned brighter. I could feel it in the house.

After the street protests, Jay broke with Sharia4Belgium for a while. He stopped going to the headquarters. I was overjoyed. Later, I learned that some of the leadership there suspected he was going to the exorcisms and other prayer sessions in people's homes to meet girls. I believe that's garbage. Jay was a handsome boy, and maybe one or two of the daughters were attracted to him. But he wasn't using Islam to meet women. He was tragically sincere about his faith.

Still, for us, it was a miracle. For ten months, Jay stayed away from the headquarters. But he was still in touch with his Muslim friends, and he still watched the videos from Iraq and Syria. Thousands of foreign fighters, from Tunisia, France, England, Russia, and the far-flung points of the globe, began to answer the call to jihad. Jay was itching to do something.

On January 29, 2013, my son turned eighteen. The clock had run out on us. He was an adult now. He controlled his own life, his own finances, his travel.

I never dreamt that Jay would leave to go fight in a foreign land. He'd never had any interest in the military; he wasn't the kind of boy who played with toy soldiers or drew tanks. The worst I thought could happen was that he would spend his life as an Islamist radical in Belgium, giving speeches on street corners, handing out pamphlets, and being a stranger to us. That was bad enough.

Soon after his birthday, Jay had a dream. In it, his friend Azzedine, the boy who'd first brought him to Sharia4Belgium, was praying for help with something. When he woke up, Jay thought about the dream. He hadn't seen Azzedine in five months. Why was he coming into his thoughts now?

A few days later, his cell phone rang. It was a foreign number he'd never seen before, beginning with the code 963. He hit "answer" and found it was Azzedine calling.

"Where are you?" Jay asked him.

"I'm in Syria."

That could only mean one thing. Azzedine had gone to fight with the rebels.

"Who else is there?"

Azzedine paused. "Everyone."

It was true. Many of the young men who'd joined Sharia-4Belgium had secretly left their homes and their families and traveled to the battlefields of Syria. Jay felt as though he'd been left behind. This was his generation's war, and he was sitting in Antwerp playing on the computer. He felt guilty.

Things happened very fast after that. Two days after their first conversation, Jay's phone rang. It was Azzedine again, asking him how much money he had. Jay told him two thousand euros. It was the money he'd received when he turned eighteen, his little savings, the birthday gifts from aunts and uncles saved up year after year, the proceeds from the little jobs he had. Now he was thinking of using it to go die for Allah.

Jay started mentioning to me and his mother that he needed to go abroad to study Arabic. *Don't you have to go to Paris to really learn French,* he said, *to get all the meanings of the language where it was born? Fine,* we said. *We'll find you a good school in Saudi Arabia or Egypt and pay for the classes. We'll even go with you!*

Again, I came off as the asshole dad who wanted to spoil the fun. Who wants to fly off on a foreign adventure with his father sitting in the next seat?

A month later, Jay told me he and his friends were planning a vacation in Holland. "Which friends?" I said. "I want to see them." He told me he would bring them by, but he never did. Secretly, he took my Samsonite suitcase and began to pack.

What could I do? You can't watch a human being every second of the day. I couldn't conceive of the possibility that Jay would run away to Syria. Yes, he was fascinated by Islam, but Syria? That was chaos, butchery. Why would he want to go there? I'd forgotten the words of my Iranian friend. He saw what I missed.

We believed Jay. We believed him because we wanted to believe him.

The idea of going to the war zone now became an actual plan. Jay went to a local store and bought a flashlight, a sleeping bag, binoculars, a camera, and winter clothes. Azzedine had told him everything he would need; Jay even went out and bought a pair of night-vision goggles. I'm sure he was excited; years before, I'd been excited to get my army gear before shipping off to Slovenia. It's fun to hold a flashlight in your hand and imagine what it will be illuminating two weeks from now, what scenes of danger and courage you're going to experience.

February 21, 2013, was an ordinary day in a not so ordinary year. My normal life was about to disappear, never to return. By the time the day's events had played out, Jay, his mother, his sister, and I would never be the same people again.

Early that morning, Jay went to the bank and took his two thousand euros out. He packed his new clothes and his sleeping bag; he forgot his passport but, luckily for him, a Belgian identity card is all you need to travel. He called Azzedine's brother, Redouan, to take him to the airport. He'd already booked a flight to Istanbul, without my knowledge.

Later, my son told me what happened next. At the airport, he turned to Redouan. "Who knows," he said, "maybe I'll see you soon. Otherwise, I'll see you in paradise."

But Jay was still a teenager. He later described to me how, after landing at the Amsterdam's Schiphol Airport on his way to Istanbul, he spotted one of his favorite things: Burger King. He went in and ordered a burger and fries. While he was savoring this last meal in the West, his flight to Istanbul was called and left without him. Such a Jay thing to do.

I can see him sitting alone at that plastic countertop, his military gear piled on the chair next to him, the flashlight and the rugged clothing stowed away. It almost brings me to tears to imagine it. I'm sure that Jay would roll his eyes at my portrayal of that moment. In his eyes, he was a man going to war; it was all very serious business. But I'm his father, and this is what I see: a boy, alone in a huge airport, missing a flight because he's excited to eat at Burger King.

Chapter Five

WE THOUGHT JAY HAD GONE to Amsterdam with his friends. It was worrying that he'd left so suddenly and without saying good-bye, and we began to call him and send him messages. A few days after he left, we got a text. He said he wasn't in Amsterdam but in Egypt. This wasn't the deal we'd agreed on. I wrote him back:

What are you doing in Egypt?

Don't worry, it's OK. I'm studying Arabic.

I took a deep breath. I'd already researched the language schools in Egypt. Some were good, but some were covers for radical groups. They advertised that they taught young foreigners the language, but in reality they were a pipeline shipping believers to the battlefields. Those schools were in the hands of extremist Salafists. I prayed he wasn't at one of them.

What school are you going to there?

No answer.

I want to come see you, I wrote.

No answer.

I racked my brains for a pretext to fly to Egypt. What would Jay believe? Egypt has great dive spots in Sharm el Sheikh. The Red Sea is a smorgasbord of wrecks and sea life. I'd always wanted to try it.

We can go diving, I typed.

Pause. *Come on, Jay.* Finally, he answered:

OK. Once I get on campus, I'll contact you.

That was the end of our little conversation. Then silence. For weeks after, we didn't hear from him. What was going on? We texted him and left voice mail messages. Nothing.

I had this nauseous feeling in my stomach as I went about my days in Antwerp. This is not my son. He knows we worry, he always calls. But not now. Something awful had entered our lives.

I couldn't sit around waiting for a miracle to happen. My son was missing. I went to the police on March 11 and tried to file a missing persons report. A female cop sat down and listened to my story. It all poured out of me: the strange behavior, the new friends, Belkacem. She took it all in with kind eyes, but at the end she told me that Jay was an adult and he could go wherever he wanted.

"But he's part of a radical organization!" I said. "Doesn't that mean anything?"

Even so, she said. If he was underage, it would be a different story.

The tension got worse. Three days later, things reached a

crescendo. It was his sister's birthday and the two of them were close. Jay would never let her birthday pass without calling her.

But the hours ticked by without a call or a text. As midnight approached, I knew that my son was gone. His sister cried, *Where's my big brother? Why didn't he call? What's happened to him?* We had that terrible feeling that he was either dead or in a situation so horrible he didn't want to tell us about it.

The stuff about Egypt was a lie, of course. Jay wasn't in Egypt. He was in Syria with his friends from Sharia4Belgium. He told me the whole story later: how he'd flown to Istanbul, Turkey, then on to the southern city of Adana. There he was to link up with two Belgian men headed for Syria. He met the men and together they jumped on a bus for Antakya, which lies just on the Turkish side of the Syrian border. Jay would say later that he expected to be dead within weeks of getting to Syria. He was going achieve martyrdom and go to paradise and meet his seventy-two virgins.

In Antakya, Jay and his two friends met a smuggler who took them to a mountain village where other fighters were gathered, looking for a chance to enter Syria. At the right moment, they crossed over, then texted their friends from Antwerp to come get them. When the car with the Sharia4Belgium members pulled up, they were all carrying an assortment of weapons. Jay was taken aback. "I asked them if this was what I had come for."

The new recruits jumped into the car and it sped off to a

small villa in a place called Kafr Hamra, where they pulled into a walled compound. This was the gathering point for jihadis who'd come from Europe. More friends arrived, including Azzedine, who had a big smile on his face. "What are you doing here?" he said to Jay jokingly. Jay stared at the shoes and boots lined up outside the villa's front door, then took his off and went in. This was his new home.

One of the first sights that met Jay was an injured Syrian jihadi. He had been wounded in battle: a few of his ribs were broken and his right leg had a gaping wound. Jay realized that the war he'd come to was real; it killed and injured people. The name of the organization he'd just joined by stepping into the villa was the Mujahideen Shura Council. "Shura" means "consultation." The group was allied with Jabhat al-Nusra, which means "The Victory Front for the People of the Levant." It was a Salafist organization that wanted to establish an Islamic State in Syria. The two groups had joined up in attacks on Assad's strongholds, including one on a military site called Base 111. After the fighters had stormed the outpost, they'd taken the army soldiers prisoner. Instead of using them for ransom or prisoner exchange, a blood sacrifice broke out and the Council members went around cutting soldiers' throats. These were the people Jay was now allied with.

The next morning, Jay began training camp. There were three parts to it: endurance training, tactics, and ideology. After morning prayer, Jay's instructors took him out for a long run, interspersed with exercises designed to strengthen his legs and upper body. This stage lasted ninety minutes. The leader of the physical training had been trained by the Egyptian special forces and knew what he was doing. After they returned to the villa, they had breakfast and then it was on to two hours of tactical work. Jay was handed an unloaded rifle and taught how it functioned. Then the training leader took the fighters out to a simulated battlefield where the jihadis make some awkward attempts to storm a number of fortified positions. They learned what to do if an enemy plane appeared in the sky and came in for the attack. Jay was taught hand signals to communicate with his brothers when the noise of battle was too loud for shouting.

Then came dinner, and after that, lectures. It was the same stuff Jay had heard back home. Some of the fighters missed the lectures, as they were outside doing guard duty.

Jay learned that, after he'd finished his training course, he'd be expected to go to the front lines once a month to fight Assad's forces. When he and his brothers weren't at the battlefield, they'd return to the villa, which had been equipped to keep young men's minds off home: Internet, PlayStations, and flat-screen TVs. One or two brothers cooked for the whole battalion; later, after they joined ISIS, that would change and food would be delivered to the camp. There was an indoor swimming pool and a fountain where water splashed.

It was almost like a resort, but it wasn't the most luxurious place in Kafr Hamra. The Arab fighters, along with a handful of Europeans, stayed in a compound called "The Palace," which was once the home of an Assad bureaucrat. It had a rooftop pool, as well as an enormous orchard.

It was a young man's war. The leader of the European fighters was a man named Houssien Elouassaki, one of the Sharia-4Belgium jihadis. He was only twenty-one years old. Most of the faces Jay saw were young. Amr al-Absi, the man with the injured leg, bought the food, clothes, fuel, and guns—but, when he was away, Elouassaki dealt with the mundane details: who cooked and did the dishes, who cleaned up the villa.

Sitting on the floor talking with the more experienced jihadis, Jay began to learn about how war was really fought. Finances, for instance. The fighters told him that, when he killed an enemy, he could take the man's belongings: his gun, money, jewelry. Some jihadis went looking for people to take prisoner so they could hold them for ransom. Others had become experts in this business, earning as much as seventy thousand euros for a single hostage. Most of the targets were Christians or Shiites. If their families couldn't come up with the money, the captives were shot in the head or beheaded with a knife. The fighters often made videos of these killings to send to the families, to shame them for not paying the ransom, and also to share among themselves.

The group set up checkpoints on the roads in and out of Kafr Hamra. When buses or cars came through, the fighters demanded that the passengers take out their wallets or purses. They studied their names for signs that the travelers were infidels: Christian, Alawi, Yazidi, Kurdish, or Shiite. They searched for crucifixes and scrolled through the pictures on mobile phones, looking for pictures of infidel shrines or Iranian ayatollahs. If any of these things were found, the person would be robbed and then ransomed. The brother of Houssien Elouassaki, Hakim, bragged about taking a gold ring from a Kurdish prisoner and stealing a computer from a Christian.

It was straight-up banditry. Hakim later recalled killing a Shiite prisoner, despite the thirty thousand euros his family had paid. "As I shot him, he put up his hand," Hakim told his girlfriend, "so the bullet went through his hand and his head." Hakim regretted only one thing about the murder. "I wish the filming worked when I killed him. I played the camera badly, and it filmed nothing." Beheadings were common; those whose family could pay nothing were forced to kneel and their heads were sawed off, sometimes with a rust-flecked machete.

The leader at Kafr Hamra was Amr al-Absi, the injured Syrian. Al-Absi had been born in Saudi Arabia but raised in Aleppo along with his dentist brother, who left for Afghanistan to fight with the Taliban. Al-Absi later joined him in the jihad and fought in Iraq before being imprisoned in Syria in 2007. After his release, and after the killing of his brother by moderate fighters, al-Absi became the leader of the Mujahideen Shura Council.

Jay also learned about taking prisoners. Most were killed immediately. In rare cases, a prisoner who showed remorse about fighting the jihadis was allowed to live. But these were exceptional situations.

While Jay was learning the ways of Kafr Hamra, I was texting him, asking if he was OK, where he was, if he would please tell his family that he wasn't suffering, if he could tell us when he was coming back. And here is when I made a mistake. A big mistake. I was casting around for solutions and one day I thought, *What about the Israelis? They seem to know everything that's happening in the Middle East. Maybe they can help.*

If I'd kept it to myself, it would have been harmless enough. But I decided to ask Jay. It wasn't a very good idea, when I look back on it. Why would the Mossad want to help a stranger, a Belgian like me? But I was crazy at the time, clutching at anything. I took out my cell phone and texted Jay. "Should I contact the Mossad? Would that help?"

I had introduced the worst possible word into Jay's life in Syria: "Mossad." For the Arab fighters, that was worse than "CIA" or "MI6." It was close to a death sentence, and now it lay waiting on Jay's screen for his brother jihadis to find.

Chapter Six

BACK IN ANTWERP, I WAS getting a little crazier with each passing day. I had no idea what had become of my son, no experience in tracking people. How do you find someone who doesn't want to be found? How do you locate someone who's disappeared into a country without a functioning government, where the people speak a strange language and those in power are hostile to your kind?

I had no idea. So I started contacting Jay's friends, including the ones in Sharia4Belgium. *Have you heard from him?* I asked them. *Do you know where he might be?* They all told me the same thing. They'd gotten no word for weeks. I texted Jay, too, more than a thousand times. No response.

I turned to the Internet. There were videos and pictures flooding out of Syria. Maybe I could spot Jay in one of them. I knew that his brothers from Sharia4Belgium were in Syria; if Jay had gone to fight, he would be with them. I looked at photos, news articles, videos, scrolling through hundreds of them a day.

It was a kind of education on Syria. Even though I was just looking for a face, I absorbed some of what was happening over there and it terrified me. I watched videos in which jihadis attacked fortified positions yelling, "Allahu Akbar!" at the tops of their voices and were martyred on camera. I saw suicide bombers give their last words. I saw many dead bodies, and for each of them I tried to make out the man's features through the streaks of blood. *Is it Jay? Has it happened already?*

Nothing. Many days I fell asleep next to my open laptop. I didn't sleep very long or very well, just a couple of hours of tossing and turning, with bad dreams populated by the faces I'd seen in the videos. I had left my job and I wasn't looking for work, I was hardly speaking to my ex-wife and daughter. I wasn't going down to my local tavern for a beer. I was like a monk searching thousands of manuscripts for the one clue that would save my son.

One day, I was trawling through YouTube when I found a video showing some fighters in Syria; they were speaking Dutch and they were standing in a field with yellow flowers with their guns by their side. As the video played, something caught my eye and I hit the pause button. On the screen, to the side of the main guys, was a young man who looked very much like Jay. I stared at the man's face for a few moments. I felt elation and worry at the same time.

His beard was a bit longer. But it was him. And he was in the place I fervently wished he wasn't. The front lines of Syria.

What to do? I'd already tried the police. I knew from reading reports that the intelligence agencies in Belgium weren't looking to rescue jihadis and bring them home. Who could I call? Doctors Without Borders? UNICEF?

I spent half a day making phone calls before I confirmed my first impressions: There was no one to help me. No organization existed for finding and retrieving fighters from ISIS. If I was to get Jay back, it was up to me.

I'm going to Syria, I thought.

There was no time to learn Arabic or do much research about the different groups in the country, but I didn't want to go to Syria totally blind. I knew that some brave journalists were covering the Civil War there and I thought my story could give their coverage a fresh twist. So I began calling around and offering to talk about my dilemma and my desire to go and find Jay. My offer was quickly accepted and I arranged for an interview with a major Belgian newspaper.

In the article, I said I was looking for someone to go with me to the country, to show me the way. Two journalists agreed—a Mexican photographer named Narciso Contreras and a female journalist, Joanie de Rijke. They had been to the Middle East before and said they had contacts in Syria who could help me find Jay. I was all for it.

I went online and booked a ticket to Turkey. I found a spare suitcase—Jay had taken my Samsonite with him—and quickly packed. I called a taxi and told the driver I was going to the airport. The agreement was that I would meet Narciso and Joanie in Turkey and we would cross the border together. It got firmed up within a couple of days. There was no time to waste.

I'm an impulsive person, I guess. I don't need a week to mull over the complexities of every move I make. Any objection that my friends raised—where will you stay, how will you avoid being kidnapped—looked small to me. Compared to what? Letting Jay die alone in a bombing or an artillery barrage? Compared to that, nothing seemed extreme or foolish.

I was afraid, but mostly of the unknown. In my Internet search for some sign of Jay, I'd come across many interviews with jihadis talking about their hatred for the West and for Westerners. It seemed I was heading to a place where everyone was going to despise me on sight. I wondered if I'd be able to deal with that hostility. I wondered if I'd be able to approach men with guns who might or might want to kill me, and keep my composure. All men think of such things when they are going into dangerous situations. *How will I measure up? What kind of a man am I, deep down?*

But on the plane, I felt something strange. After the weeks of terrible uncertainty, I was happy. It was odd; I was heading to a war zone where innocent civilians were dying alongside the soldiers on both sides, but I felt no fear. I was taking action. I felt my love for Jay making me strong; it covered me like a bulletproof cloak.

Meanwhile, in Syria, the brutality of the fighters was beginning to unnerve Jay. Where were the innocent Muslims he had come to protect? What he was seeing seemed closer to gang warfare than holy war, with the Sunnis versus the Christians and the Shiites. After finishing the first part of his training, Jay was handed a headband with "Mujahideen Shura Council" printed in white on the black cloth. He expected he would be wearing it when he died at the front lines.

Jay, however, refused to go. He wasn't here to kill Shiites or members of other Islamic militias. He was feeling down about the journey he'd made. Around this time, his sinuses became infected and he visited a hospital. While the doctor was treating him, Jay asked the man to give him a prescription for antidepressants.

My son had never taken such things before. That he was looking for mood-altering drugs says to me that Syria was a complete shock to him. He realized he'd been lied to.

Jay knew that, if he stayed in Syria, he would be expected to take part in the beheadings and the rest of the horrible shit that was going down. He didn't want that, so he screwed up his courage and asked one of the top-ranking fighters if he could go home to Belgium. When the man asked him why, Jay said he wasn't well; he needed medical treatment. The jihadi said he had no problem with Jay leaving. But Houssien Eloussaki, the head of his fighting unit, refused to hear of it, and instantly regarded Jay with suspicion. Why had he come all this way, spent all this money, just to turn around and go back? He insisted that Jay turn over his Belgian identity card and his cell phone. Jay gave him the card but told him he didn't have his phone with him.

The training continued. One morning, March 5, Jay sat down for breakfast with Azeddine and Houssien. After they'd finished, the two men turned on him: They tied his hands and forced him to walk up a hill. There they shoved him inside a bunker that served as the brigade's prison. Inside, they chained his hands to a wall. Jay asked what he'd done wrong but the fighters refused to answer him. Meanwhile, they found his phone and began scrolling through the messages. There they came across the messages from me, one of which had the word "Mossad" in it.

I can't imagine what Jay was feeling at this moment. He thought he'd found a way to serve his fellow man—at least his fellow Muslims—and had given himself to the cause fully. Now he was being treated like a Judas, when the only thing he'd done wrong was have a few doubts about the mission his fellow fighters were embarked on. He'd thought for himself. But in Syria, that was enough.

Rumors began to circulate about my son. Anyone who came here not to fight must be a spy. What else would he be doing in Kafr Hamra?

Chapter Seven

I MET JOANIE AND NARCISO in Istanbul and we proceeded immediately toward the Syrian border. Narciso was in his late thirties, thin, quiet, and intense-looking, with hair that now and then swept over his eyes. He was a top war photographer with a haunting style who'd traveled all over the world shooting scenes of conflict. Joanie was in her late forties, with a round face and long blond hair. In 2008, she'd been kidnapped by the Taliban and suffered through a horrible experience, including being raped by one of the group's leaders. She was experienced, and tough as hell.

Together, we waited for a chance to cross into Syria, and it finally arrived in early April. When our guides told us we'd passed the border, I felt a surge of adrenaline. *Now I am in the same country as my son. It's as if he was a beacon to me, sending strength my way.*

We made our way to Aleppo in northwest Syria. Before the war, it was the largest city in Syria, bigger than Damascus, and for centuries was an important trading center in the Ottoman Empire. Its roots go back to the sixth century B.C. We drove quickly down the streets, to avoid snipers, so I only saw flashes of the city through the dusty windows of our car. But what I saw— sand-colored minarets, beautiful apartment buildings, bustling street life—made it seem like a prosperous city on an ordinary day. Only the gunfire in the distance and the occasional detonation of a shell told me I was near the front lines of a civil war.

The two journalists were as good as their word: they knew some rebel fighters, and they promised that in the morning they would introduce me to them. Then my search for my boy would begin in earnest. The fighters would be the key; they knew where the foreigners were. They might even have run into Jay in their travels to distant battlefields.

That first night we slept in a room with some Free Syrian Army fighters who'd agreed to help us. I couldn't believe it. I thought Muslims hated people like me, but on my first day in Syria, I already had a place to stay. *Would that happen in Antwerp?* I thought. I was a reverse migrant; thousands of Syrians were crossing the Mediterranean Sea and crowding into boats to make a perilous trip to Europe, and they were not being welcomed. Here I was, going the other way, and I found kindness and shelter immediately. I was moved by that.

It was late. Around me, people were lying on mats or on the bare concrete. Some snored quietly. I couldn't sleep. I could hear the sound of artillery and of bombs hitting not too far away. I could feel the pressure waves on my skin. The fighting sounded very heavy and very close now. I'm sure it was farther away than

I imagined; if we'd truly been in danger, wouldn't the guys around me have gotten up and hustled us out of the building?

I nudged Narciso, who was lying next to me.

"Narciso," I said.

His eyes were closed and his breath was making a light whistling sound as he fell into a deep sleep.

"Narciso."

His eyes opened and he looked over at me.

"Yes?"

"Are you sure it's safe to stay here?"

He smiled.

"It's fine, Dimitri," he whispered. "Go to sleep."

The next morning, I woke up after a couple of hours of fitful rest. My back ached. For breakfast, Narciso, Joanie, and I sat in a circle with the rebels and ate hummus and long strings of goat cheese, along with salad and tomatoes. There was no meat at all to speak of. Belgians love meat; half our diet consists of it. But it would be a while before I tasted it again. Still, after a long night, the food was fresh and tasted good. I thanked them for it.

I saw that the fighters lived rough. There were no utensils for the food; you ate with your hands. The bathroom was a hole in the floor. But I was here and I was happy.

I had brought a picture of Jay and, after breakfast, we got in a car and began our scouting. How do you find a single man in a chaotic battle-torn country where records have been destroyed and no one trusts anyone else? You have to rely on the human touch. You have to let people see the love and desperation in your eyes. It's the only way.

I knocked on doors. Literally. That first day we got a lead on a battalion that had run across some foreigners. "They're staying four blocks away," a fighter told us. "Go and see them."

Was it a trap? My pale face was already getting sunburned, but the very whiteness of it stuck out.

I went to the villa with Narciso and Joanie and our driver. We made small talk on the way, but I was nervous. When we got to the place, a battered villa on a side street in eastern Aleppo, I knocked on the door. A fighter came to the door and invited me in. It was a room like the one I'd left, some thin mattresses and bedrolls on the floor, dirty dishes, an old TV. And young men.

We sat down in a circle on the floor. Most of the fighters spoke some English or French. I was able to explain my mission. Simple words, but effective.

But first, tea. Nothing happened in Syria without tea. And food. Initially, I was grateful for Arab hospitality. Later, I would wish we could just cut straight to the talking.

Narciso had told me what to look for. If the fighters were wearing jeans and sneakers, they were most likely cool. That is, they weren't Salafists who wanted to cut the head off any Westerner they saw. If I saw a cigarette in someone's hand, I immediately relaxed. If they were smoking tobacco, they weren't hard-line.

Over tea and some hummus, I told them my story. I was a father looking for my son. I had reason to believe he wanted to come home. (I made that part up—I didn't want to look like someone who'd come to take back a devoted jihadi). I was alone and depending on Syrians to help me. Would they look at the picture I'd brought?

The leader of the group smiled. "Of course," he said. I handed the picture to him and he studied it closely, as if he was memorizing the features. But after about thirty seconds, he shook his head and passed it to the next guy. Fighters leaned over his shoulder to take a look and they made some comments in Arabic.

The photo made the rounds. Nobody had seen my son. My heart sank a bit, but I hadn't expected to hit pay dirt on the first day. I knew this would be an odyssey. I was so right.

We got back in the car and started driving through Aleppo. The city was coming alive: shoppers on the street, women—some with their faces veiled, some with a scarf across their shoulders but their heads bare. I was stunned by the ancient structures: the citadels, the mosques, the arched tunnels built of stone that ran through the city. It looked like one of the places I would have come to visit when I was young: an old, mystical place. But then I'd see a group of men with RPGs slung over their shoulders.

I saw apartment buildings that had collapsed in on themselves, their fronts blown off and the floors tumbled one on the other like Jenga blocks. We passed one structure that looked like a huge fist had come down on the roof and smashed everything into a jumble of concrete, rebar, and furniture.

"What is that place?" I asked the driver.

He looked over. "Hospital."

I was shocked. Where would the people go now who were

wounded or injured? It was clear that, with this many apartment buildings demolished, there were many casualties. But Assad had not only bombed Aleppo's people, he'd bombed the places that would help them if they were hurt. It was cruelty on a level I hadn't seen in Slovenia.

Two things were good for instant bonding in Syria: guns and cigarettes. Guns would come later. But I'm a smoker and seeing fellow smokers relaxed me: at least I'd be able to get a fix in Syria, I thought. When I saw the distinctive red and white of Marlboro boxes in their pockets, I was overjoyed. That was my brand. Fighters shared their tobacco with me, but I soon learned that not everything was as it seemed. The cigarettes were fake; I knew it as soon as I put one to my lips. My body was crying out for good Virginia tobacco. Later, I would drag Narciso and Joanie and our little entourage all over Aleppo until we found an authentic carton in a small shop. I paid some ungodly fortune to buy the carton, but I was in heaven.

But for now, I had to smoke this garbage. The cigarette thing became a running joke.

"Hey, Dimitri, did you find your Marlboros?"

"No."

"Here, have one of mine."

I took one.

"This is shit, Abdul."

And they would laugh.

Beards, on the other hand, made me nervous. Djellabas, too.

And, especially, balaclavas. These were the hats that pulled down over the face, leaving only room for the eyes and the mouth. A balaclava meant one thing: I don't want to be identified because what I'm doing is crazy. Out of bounds. If I saw a balaclava with a beard extending out beneath it, my knees went weak for a moment. That was a bad dude.

Those first days, I was a curiosity. "What are you doing here?" fighters would say. "Journalist? Aid worker?"

"No. I'm just a father. I've come looking for my son."

This stopped them. "Your son?"

"His name is Jay, he's from Belgium. He ran away and I want to get him back. Will you help me?"

The Arabs I came across, most of them anyway, were incredibly generous. The father-son bond in Arab culture is strong, close to sacred. Secretly, I think many believed that Western families didn't cherish their children in the way Arabs did. Western families were a little distant, a little cold. So when they saw a Westerner come, unarmed, to rescue his child, it struck a chord in them. Many of them had left their own families behind in other parts of Syria to come fight. They felt a connection to me.

But it wasn't just the fact that I'd come to Syria at the risk of my own life. There was something else. It was the fact that Jay had been a member of a Christian family and then became a Muslim. In Islamic families, the thought of sons changing faith was something almost unimaginable. In the West, it can be a big deal, too, of course. At first, I didn't understand Jay's decision and we had plenty of arguments about it. But I believe it's up to each human being to find his path in the world, and they have the right to choose it. Who was I to stand in the way of a heartfelt conversion?

For the fighters and activists I spoke to, this was astounding. "He changed his religion, and you were OK with this?"

"Well, yes, after a while."

They loved that Jay had become a Muslim, but in their culture, they expected me, as a Christian, to disown my child. For them, the chasm between Islam and Christianity was un-bridgeable. They were grateful that I'd accepted Islam into my family.

This wasn't enough, of course. Most of the fighters I met wanted me to become a Muslim, too, especially when I told them I was an atheist. (For some reason, it was safer to tell the Salafist fighters I was an atheist; the secular fighters I would tell I was Christian—"Syria rules," I called it). "Dimitri," the Salafists would say. "Allah has led you to Syria after your son. Perhaps this is a message. Why don't you accept Islam?"

I wanted to laugh. My introduction to Islam hadn't been all that . . . attractive, shall we say. Plus, I loved whiskey, cigarettes, dancing, and, now that I was single, sleeping with strange women. I wanted to say, "I didn't made it as a Christian. What makes you think I would do any better as a Muslim?" But the expressions on these guys were dead serious, and I knew enough not to kid around on this subject.

Even the secular fighters asked me why I didn't convert. I lis-tened to them and heard the good version of the worldwide caliphate that Jay had been seduced by. They spoke of one people all around the world, one leader, one religion. They felt they were trying to tell me something valuable that would open up my life to happiness. One sheikh, when he prayed, would use a small vial of perfume as part of the ritual. One afternoon, before he knelt down, he took a drop on his fingertip and tapped my shoulder. "Dimitri," he said, "why don't you become a Muslim?"

He was an important guy. I thought he might be useful in the future.

"First my son," I said. "And then we'll talk about it."

One jihadi intellectual published an article called "Why We Hate You & Why We Fight You." One passage in it goes like this: "We fight you, not simply to punish and deter you, but to bring you true freedom in this life and salvation in the Hereafter, freedom from being enslaved to your whims and desires as well as those of your clergy and legislatures, and salvation by worshipping your Creator alone and following his Messenger." That was a good summary of what I heard again and again in Syria. The jihadis had a lot in common with the Seventh-day Adventists and Mormons who go around knocking on people's doors and asking them if they've seen the light. Only the Islamists believed that violence was an acceptable way to get you to see that light.

Even though there was no chance I was going to be praying five times a day toward Mecca, I was moved by their concern for my soul. Really. How many people in the West ask about your spiritual life after talking you for ten minutes? But behind it, I felt the same thing my son had gone through: that insistence that Islam was the one true way. And behind that lay something far more sinister: the global caliphate achieved through coercion and pain. Created in moments like these, one convert at a time.

But fighters listened to my story. Their eyes softened. They touched their open palm over their hearts and said, "Inshallah, I will do whatever I can." A few of them were snakes, only after my money, but many of them meant it. And would put their lives on the line to back it up. If I made a list of all the Arab men and women who helped me, it would run into the hundreds. And I owe each of them a debt that's written on my heart.

Chapter Eight

DAY AFTER DAY, WE WENT all over Aleppo looking for Jay. The checkpoints were the worst part. That's where the danger was. I always sat in back with Narciso and Joanie while, in front, our driver and a rebel fighter who was acting as our guide would field all the questions.

Each rebel group had its own flag or banner. In the car that we hired, we kept a supply of them in the backseat. When we passed from one territory to another, we would get out and tie the new flag to the rearview mirror. It became like a game. "Stop the car! Where are we entering now?" There were flags for the Free Syrian Army, Liwa al Tawhid, and al-Nusra.

Most streets at night were deserted; the checkpoints were far more dangerous at night, with the guards nervous on their triggers. Some people drove around with night-vision glasses, as the streetlights were often out and the electricity in the buildings, too. If you drove at night, you raced through this dead landscape filled with dark buildings. If you used your headlights, you could become a target for a sniper, so people drove with their lights out, moving at 50 or 60 mph. I tried only to be in cars during the daytime. That was dangerous enough for me.

I did my best to dress like a jihadi. I wore a keffiyeh, the black-and-white Palestinian scarf, around my neck. We would go to a checkpoint and a guy with a Kalashnikov would ask the translator, "Who are these people?"

The guy would point to me.

"He's looking for his son."

Stares.

"Where is this son?"

"That's what we're trying to find out."

Most times, they waved us on. Other times, we had to turn around. People thought I was a spy coming to look at rebel positions and relay them back to Assad's planes. It didn't help that I happen to look a little Russian. The Russians were on the wrong side of this war.

The third day, I went to the headquarters of a Salafist group. I was terrified. These were the people who were chopping off people's heads. It was a normal villa in eastern Aleppo, which is more conservative than the western part. We pulled up to this buff-colored house, with two guards outside. They were wearing black djellabas and balaclavas.

Despite my determination, I felt a cold shudder run through me. These guys brought back memories of videos I'd seen. And many others. The killers always wore balaclavas.

Everything I was doing went against my military training. I was unarmed. I didn't know these people I was going to meet.

Totally against protocol. Was I walking into a trap with my eyes wide open?

"Do you think it's safe?" I asked one of the activists in English as I stepped out of the car.

"If you believe in Allah," he said, "don't be afraid."

It's something people say in the Middle East, like when your plane goes through turbulence or your car is broken down in a dangerous neighborhood, but in the current situation it wasn't very comforting. *I don't believe in Allah,* I wanted to say. *That's the point. So yeah, not very helpful.*

We went inside. There was a main living room and young men were lounging on the sofas. They, too, wore black djellabas and balaclavas. Some were cleaning their weapons. Others were glancing at the news on an Arab channel.

There was something in the air . . . it's hard to describe. I felt like I was stepping onto an alien planet. These guys didn't seem 100 percent human. There was hostility mixed with the oxygen. They were like Islamic robots and they fed on hatred of people like me. I didn't feel that traditional Arab welcome that I'd grown to appreciate.

I sat on the floor. The emir, a bulky guy with a black beard bordered with red, eyed me. This would be the point, in a normal Arab home, when he would offer me food. But not here.

"You are the father?" he said in Arabic.

"Yes," I said, trying to sound more confident than I was. "I've come to find my son."

The eyes of the men near him bore into mine.

"Belgians," the emir said. "What do I have to do with Belgians?"

I shrugged.

"I'm looking for information, that's all."

"We don't know anything about your son. Do not come here again."

And that was that. Stonewalled. We got out of there as fast as we could.

I quickly sensed something about Syria. It was a man's world. Not only that, it was a man's man's world. These were tough guys. I wasn't in Belgium anymore, where men sipped wine, carried briefcases made of thin leather, wore Burberry shirts, and chatted about the latest foreign film. This was the frontier and I'd better start acting like it.

I had to be like them.

Those first days, men came up to me and showed me their weapons. Everywhere you looked there was another kind of gun: AK-47s, M16 rifles, rocket-propelled grenades, Beretta handguns, Smith & Wessons left over from the American invasion, Colts, Sig Sauers, mortars, small handguns from Eastern Europe. It was like a gun show from one end of the country to another.

In Belgium, your tie might be an icebreaker. *Hey, great tie, where'd you get it? Hugo Boss, right? Nice! Do they have it in periwinkle?* In Syria, it's your weapon. Rebels wanted me to hold their guns, to feel the weight of them, check out how badass they were. It was like being back in the army. Everyone and his brother was a gun geek.

I hoisted their guns, talked about them. *What's the range of this thing, brother? You must be shitting me! No way it hits a target at that distance!* Their eyes lit up, you better believe it. Here in Babel, guns were a common language.

I saw amazing things in Syria. I saw a fighter using a wooden magazine to load bullets into his AK-47. It was handcrafted— I'd never seen that before. I visited the little workshops where the rebels made their bombs out of household goods. There were slingshots made out of rope and metal; video game controllers used to shoot mortar rounds; missiles made from scratch in metal-working shops; homemade grenades. Not to mention "tanks" fashioned out of regular trucks and covered with sheets of metal welded onto the frame. After the government planes dropped their bombs, the rebels would go out and scour the landscape for unexploded munitions, then bring them back to their little factories, extract the explosives and reuse the components. It was dangerous as all hell, but the only way to get top-grade explosives.

Whatever you thought of their ideology, it was just cool to see such ingenuity in the resistance. These people would not give up.

I even found, much to my own shock, armaments that had been made in Belgium. It happened when one fighting group took me to their "weapons room." It was just a bedroom inside a normal apartment building, but when I walked in, it was wall-to-wall guns. There were even racks on the wall you could slip a rifle onto.

It reminded me of the movies, of course. Films like *Mission: Impossible* where the good guys flick a switch and a wall slides open, *whoosh,* to show this incredible selection of pistols and hand grenades. Weapons of all shapes and sizes. Cool blue lighting. Tom Cruise picks them up one after another and chooses his favorite. There's usually some groovy music to go along with the scene. I love *Mission: Impossible.*

Here, there was just a normal light bulb and no music. But the selection of weapons was fantastic. Russian, American, some beat-up, some fairly new. And then I saw my old gun on the wall.

It was an FNC, a 45mm NATO assault rifle made by the Belgian company FN Herstal, the same weapon I'd carried in Slovenia. I was shocked to see it here in Aleppo. It was like coming across a piece of my youth in the most unexpected place. I picked up the weapon and turned it over to look at the serial number, but it had been filed off.

I felt disgusted. *How did this get here?* I wondered. Was my own country somehow supplying weapons to the fighters? My government hadn't been able to give me the slightest help in finding Jay, but here was one of our best guns contributing to the killing. Brilliant.

So yeah, I posed with AK-47s pointed at the sky and tried to look like a mercenary. Later on, I even recorded a video with some Syrian rebels, where I fired a Kalashnikov at the sky and joined in their cries of "Allahu Akbar!" When later, those pictures ran in the European press, I came in for a lot of criticism. *Look at these photos! Bontinck's become one of the mujahideen!*

My intention wasn't to glorify the armed rebellion; it was

simply to win the confidence of the rebels, whom I needed for information and to draw attention to the plight of my son. Honestly, I would have gotten in a tank and shot a round off if it would have gotten me closer to Jay. When you're in Rome, you speak Italian. When you're in Syria, you mess around with guns. You walk tall. You look men in the eye. If you show fear to the fighters, they will lose interest in you. Men who risk their lives every day are not interested in soft people. If you look like you're terrified of getting shot, they won't give you the time of day.

I even had a T-shirt that helped. I'd bought it in the U.S. while on vacation years before. It's a brown shirt with a laughing skull on it. For some reason, everyone in Syria loved that shirt. "Before I talked to you," said one Free Syrian Army fighter, "I thought you were a terrorist."

"A terrorist!" I laughed. "Why?"

"That T-shirt," he said. "It's crazy!"

Anything to show I wasn't a victim waiting to be kidnapped. It's good to be feared a little. Sympathy only takes you so far.

Chapter Nine

ON THE FIFTH DAY, I met a rebel who'd been all over northern Syria. I told him about my son. He had a bandolier of bullets across his shoulders and a weary air about him. I showed him the photos.

"You should go to Kafr Hamra," the man said. He seemed exhausted.

It was the first time I'd heard of this place.

"Where is that?"

"Fifteen kilometers north."

"Why should I go there?"

The guy shrugged his shoulders. "You said your son is Belgian?"

I nodded.

"Well, that's where the Belgians are."

I told my driver about this. His face fell.

"Ah, Kafr Hamra," he said. "Bad place."

"Why bad?"

"Dangerous."

I put it aside for the moment. I was hearing all kinds of things from the rebels. I needed to get more information.

In the next days, I kept scouring neighborhoods, talking to people on street corners, meeting activists. "Have you seen a European? Can you look at this picture?" I was a traveling salesman. All I was lacking was the suitcase with my brushes in it.

I was amazed by many things in Syria. Normal life went on as everywhere else in the world, even with helicopters dropping barrel bombs. Along with the fighters dripping with grenades, you would see scenes of the most ordinary life. Families heading out at dusk to get some ice cream. Young people walking around, flirting with each other. You would turn a corner and there would be kids playing a game of soccer with an ancient, scuffed-up ball.

Some of the food tasted fresher, especially the tomatoes. I've never had a tomato that equaled the ones I had in Aleppo. And the night sky was incredible; with the electricity cuts, you could see the stars clearly in the darkness, as if they were shapes cut into a dark piece of metal with a bright light behind it. It felt sometimes, in the more deserted parts of Syria, that you were in a desert caravan like travelers a hundred years before, looking to the stars for guidance.

Then the women. Most of them wore black abayas so that all you could see was their eyes. I always looked to their eyes. Maybe the Islamic dress increased the fascination for me, simply because the person underneath was totally unknowable except for the expression in their eyes. *What do they look like?* you wonder. *What are their lives like? Are they married, single, happy, angry, funny or not?* I must admit that when their eyes were particularly beautiful, I wondered what they looked like under the abaya.

I was walking along the street when one of the activists I'd met said something to me. "Stop looking at them," he said.

I knew what he meant immediately, of course.

"Why?" I didn't consider my glances to be offensive. I was curious.

"It's forbidden to look them in the eye."

I shook my head. Was I supposed to pretend these women didn't exist? Was it more acceptable to look at their bodies?

The fact that I was searching for my son made it possible for me to talk to some of these women. If they'd come from outside Aleppo, I'd ask: How many checkpoints did you come through? Were you stopped? Which fighting group is in control there? I found them easy to talk to, just as curious about me as I was about them.

I had the feeling that many of the women were friendlier toward Westerners than the fighters. This was their home and they were fed up with the war. They never asked me questions, and their husbands would listen closely to me to make sure I wasn't saying anything improper. But I rarely met one who was hostile or who refused to talk to me.

The women in the more secular, western neighborhoods of Aleppo often wore jeans and colorful scarves across their shoulders or over their hair. They were beautiful, with their brown eyes and their eyebrows dark against their skin. Sexy. But I hadn't thought of sex since Jay had disappeared, to be honest. I was too depressed and anxious. And when I entered Syria I assumed my romantic life was on hold. This was a conservative Muslim society, not Miami Beach.

But when I met one female activist in Aleppo, my interest in women was instantly rekindled. She was a member of a rebel group who opposed Assad. She spoke English, she was approachable, had long blond hair, which is rare in Syria, chestnut-brown eyes, and big breasts. As we talked about the regime and about the situation on the roads, and where it was safe to travel and where it was a no-go zone, I got this odd feeling. She smiled when I talked. She nodded. After a few moments, I realized I was flirting with her.

Is this wise? I asked myself. *This could get you shot. This could get* her *shot also.*

But I didn't stop. When this woman circulated among the small group of activists I was talking to, my eyes would follow her. It was as if they had a mind of their own. I couldn't look away.

I needed to buy some cigarettes. A perfect excuse. I asked the woman if she would walk with me to one of the neighborhood shops. We strolled that way, and I felt a buried excitement as we went. It felt natural being with her. All the other women in Syria I'd met, I felt like I was walking with an activist or a housewife and nothing else. But here, I felt like I was walking with a woman.

I'm not sure what's happening here, I thought. *This is forbidden! I should stop this right now.*

But the more I thought about not doing it, the more I wanted to do it.

We came out of the shop with my pack of fake Marlboros and I said, the hell with it. I leaned in and kissed her. She didn't pull away or anything; instead she pressed her lips to mine. This was in broad daylight on a street in western Aleppo. I couldn't believe how stupid we were being. But damn, it felt good.

I needed to take this inside, for her sake. The penalty for being with a man who isn't your husband is stoning. She was in more danger than I.

We walked back to the room where I was staying. It was the middle of the day and the place was deserted. In one of the rooms was a real bed. I led her to it and began to kiss her again. I felt my heart began to bump faster as I closed the door behind us. I said to myself, *This is not happening. You are asleep in a room full of snoring men, and this is your erotic dream.*

But it did happen. And the sex was great. There was no love affair, no words, nothing about the future. Maybe it was the fact that we would both have been punished severely if anyone found us, or maybe it was that the violence we saw all around us inspired a need to reaffirm life at its most basic. Explain it away any way you like, but it was fantastic. Afterward, we laughed and chatted as if we were old friends. I felt refreshed, like I was human again after all the pain of losing my son. It was almost a mystical feeling, like some part of me had been restored.

Why did this woman sleep with me? I've thought about that often since I left Syria. I'm sure part of it was because being with a Western guy was a bit of an adventure for her. It was forbidden, and forbidden things are exciting. Maybe she was sick of being dictated to in her personal life, maybe this was a big fuck-you to the extremists. I didn't care, honestly. I was just grateful it had happened.

I never saw that woman again. But that afternoon in Aleppo will stay with me until I'm old and no longer think of such things.

More and more, I was hearing the name "Kafr Hamra." My guides didn't want to go there. But I began to feel that, after this leap into the unknown, I was marking time. I needed to go to Kafr Hamra and see if my son had been there.

And so I went. With my heart in my throat. And the disaster I'd been dreading happened.

We took the same car we'd been using for the last two weeks, and Narciso and Joanie and I made small talk in the back.

"What if you meet him," Narciso said. "And he doesn't want to come home?"

"He will come," I said.

"Many don't," Narciso said, shaking his head. We'd had this conversation before.

I thought about it. "Then I'll be grateful to see his face, to touch him," I said. But was that really true? I didn't know if I could walk away and leave Jay in this place.

The guards at the checkpoint outside of Kafr Hamra seemed on edge. One of them walked around the car and studied us closely in the back seat. And when he asked his questions to the driver, his voice was harsh, biting. I could feel my gut tighten up.

The same hostility I'd felt in that room full of masked Salafists, I felt here.

We made it to the villa and I got out. I felt I'd come to the right place. Kafr Hamra was the name I'd heard more than any other and now I was here.

I took off my shoes and entered the villa. Then there was the brief interview with the emir. I was getting ready to explain my mission in more detail, to begin a long conversation

Then that unforgettable feeling of a hood being pulled over my head. Instantly, I felt claustrophobic. As I was pushed toward the basement with my hands behind my back, I said to myself, *You've made a horrible mistake.*

I struggled to control my breathing. Panic and the blows to my sides and chest made it hard to get any air. After the first few moments, the beating got worse. Every time I denied I was a spy, they hit me harder. I was crouched on my knees and blows were raining down from every direction.

You are here for your son, I thought. *Love wins out over hate.*

But what if I'd come to the one place on earth where it wouldn't?

I heard someone shouting in my ear. "You're lying. You're a filthy Zionist spy and we're going to cut off your head."

I tried to protest, but I didn't realize this wasn't an interrogation. It was an organized beating. A boot slammed into my rib cage. I felt I was choking inside the black hood.

Then the blows stopped. The jihadists yelled to me that they were searching my phone for any contacts with the police. "If we find even one," said a voice, "we're going to kill you."

What police? I thought. *In Belgium?* Then I am as good as dead. Because of course I was in touch with them. I didn't know what they were talking about.

Through the cloth, I could still see the bright light. It seemed to follow me, a light halo in the blackness. They were making a video, I was sure of it.

A hand grabbed the back of my head, gripping the cloth of the hood. It tilted my head back and I felt something being shoved into my mouth. I gagged and tried to turn away, but the hands steadied my head. It tasted bitter, like metal. I realized it was the barrel of a Kalashnikov.

"Now, Mossad spy, you tell us how you came here."

I gagged on the rifle snout. I couldn't get my tongue around it to form words.

"What? What are you saying?"

I tilted my head back, freeing up a little room. I gasped out a reply. "I'm not a spy. I came here to find my son."

The end of the barrel dug into the flesh of my tongue. "Only Allah decides if your son stays in Syria. You shouldn't interfere in these things."

Was that a confirmation that Jay was here, in Kafr Hamra? To tell you the truth, it was only a fleeting thought. I was focused on my survival now.

I began to lose consciousness. I said to myself, *Is it all worth this?* The pain was excruciating; it was getting difficult to breathe with my cracked ribs. I said to myself, *I believe in my son, there is love for my son. If there is any God, they will release me.*

I couldn't say anything. The rifle snout was pinning my

tongue to the floor of my mouth. Saliva backed up in my throat and I gagged. I tried to mumble a few words, but it was gibberish. I heard laughter.

The mood in the room was changing. Perhaps the men realized I had no information to provide. One of them pulled me up to my feet. Others began to shout commands to me.

"You are a chicken!" someone cried.

I said nothing.

"You are a chicken, act like a chicken." The hands released me.

"What?" I said, my voice a croak.

I stood there. I had a feeling they weren't going to kill me. But they wanted something else, to humiliate me.

A hand slapped the hood. My lip stung, and I tasted blood in my mouth. Still, I did nothing.

"Act like a chicken." The voice was more insistent now. The laughter had gone out of it.

A blow to my stomach. I crouched over.

"Now!"

I closed my eyes. I wasn't going to get out of here with my dignity intact. I had to accept that. Better to live and save Jay than to worry about my honor.

I clucked. My throat was dry and it came out as a cackle.

"What the fuck is this? I said *chicken*." A fist slammed into my right eye through the hood.

I tried to wet my tongue. I clucked again. I began to move around the floor, shuffling like a chicken. Laughter.

"Now a goat."

I felt a hot flush creep up my throat; my face stung. I wanted to rip an AK-47 out of the hands of one of these fuck-heads and mow down the whole room. I could sense how the AK would feel in my hands, the almost gentle recoil and push forward as it ejected round after round.

The calls came from all around me. "Monkey!" "Horse!" I shifted into different positions, doing a basic imitation of the animals. The laughter came back, this time raucous.

This went on for what seemed like hours. I don't know how long it was, really; I lost all sense of time. I was exhausted, sweat poured down my forehead. Then, finally, someone slipped a key into my handcuffs and opened them. The hood was pulled off.

I was in a basement, with six or seven jihadis gathered around me. The walls were in darkness, but it looked like bare cement. The men still had their balaclavas on. Whatever video camera they'd been using was no longer in sight.

The men let me dress, talking among themselves as I pulled on my clothes. I felt barely able to function; my arms and legs were weak. Some of the fighters went up the stairs. I followed with two jihadis beside me.

In the living room, the emir had gone. A couple of fighters were sitting on the couches; they looked at me with no interest in their eyes. The others sat me down and served me some tea. They asked if I wanted bread, hummus. I shook my head.

It was bizarre. *Now* they were trying to be hospitable? I drank the tea as fast as I could, then stood up. The men seemed to believe they'd treated me well, that everything had been done properly. They handed me back my passport and led me outside toward the car, baking in the sun.

"Don't come back here," one of them said as I got into the car.

Later, I found out that while I was in the basement, fighters had come out of the villa and beat my Syrian driver and threatened him with beheading. The same for Narciso. It had all come very close to ending in tragedy.

As we pulled away, I looked back at the walled villa. I wished I could drive a tank straight through it. I would have liked to crush the bodies of these men—not because they had tortured me, but because they did it to an innocent, unarmed man who was on a peaceful mission. That I could not forgive.

The incident in the basement seemed like the end of my mission. I couldn't know then that I'd come very close to Jay; that Amr al-Absi was his emir and that, in the moment I was suffering in the basement, he was only yards away in his bunker prison.

I felt like the life had been drained out of me. I was on the wrong path. All I'd found in Syria were some rumors and that horror in Kafr Hamra.

I began to notice something. Many of the young fighters reacted badly to Joanie's presence. To have a single, unaccompanied woman along with me emphasized that I was a Westerner. No Syrian would do such a thing. And another thing: Narciso and Joanie knew rebels, as they said they did, but only low-level ones. Their contacts were the young jihadis. I needed to talk to emirs, to generals, men in power whose intelligence networks spread far and wide. Even though they had gotten me to Aleppo, my mission was going nowhere. We were stuck.

I called my lawyer Kris in Belgium. He told me they'd arrested Fouad Belkacem and charged him with being part of a terrorist organization. I was ecstatic.

"It's time to come home," he told me.

I was running out of money. I had no good new leads. I'd learned a lot from Narciso and Joanie, but it was time to move on. I was grateful for their help but I needed to reach higher, to talk to decision makers. I decided to go back to Belgium and start planning for a second trip. I also wanted to publicize Jay's case, to put pressure on whichever fighting group he was with.

"For now," I told Kris. "But I'm coming back."

I left Joanie and Narciso and headed for the town of Kilis in Turkey. There I rented a hotel room. As soon as I closed the door behind me and locked it, I began stripping off my clothes. I got into the shower and turned it on full blast. Hot water cascaded down over me for the first time in many weeks. It was blissful. I spent an hour in the shower. I've never taken a hot shower for granted since.

But after I'd toweled off and sat on the bed, I felt the first clouds of depression wash over me. I'd left Syria without my son. I felt as though I'd left part of myself back in Aleppo. *Where is he?* I kept asking myself. *Is he even still alive?*

My son had become a ghost.

Chapter Ten

BACK IN KAFR HAMRA, FIGHTERS kept walking up the hill from the walled villa to the bunker prison to question Jay. After my visit, the questions got sharper and more insistent. Was he sending secret messages to people on the outside targeting Kafr Hamra? And what was this message from abroad that mentioned Mossad? This they were especially angry about.

Finally, the door to his prison cell opened and Amr al-Absi himself appeared. He shuffled into the room on his crutches. Jay was terrified. Had a decision on his life been reached?

"Abu Assya," al-Absi said, using my son's Islamist nickname. "I need to know something. Did you seek assistance from Israel?"

Jay was stunned. Al-Absi was, of course, referring to my unfortunate message about Mossad. What trouble that little text had caused! Jay knew that if he admitted being in touch with Mossad in any way, he would be taken out and shot. "I told him that this was one big mistake," Jay said.

Al-Absi looked at Jay, then left. After a few days, Jay heard the verdict on his fate. He was to be released, so long as he agreed to finish his training and pledge his loyalty to the battalion. This meant that he had to fight. Jay agreed. Anything to get out of that prison on the hill.

Jay rejoined the fighting group and resumed his training. One night, after their exercises, a fellow Belgian fighter was talking with Jay. He told my son that, to be honest, he was feeling increasingly homesick. Syria had not turned out the way he expected, and he was thinking of escaping and making his way back to Belgium. Would Jay help?

My son said he felt the same way. Not only would he help his fellow jihadi, he would go with him out of the camp and back to Europe. For the first time in many weeks, Jay felt hopeful. He was going to correct his mistake. He was heading home.

The two planned their escape in detail. One night, when the stars and moon were out and the camp was quiet, the Belgian jihadi and Jay grabbed their belongings and made their way out of the villa. No one stopped them. Jay's heart was in his throat. It was actually happening.

Then, out of nowhere, a BMW sedan with Belgian plates roared up and stopped in front of the two fighters. Jihadis jumped out and grabbed Jay. The other fighter only smiled at him. Jay had been set up.

The other fighters cursed Jay and bundled him into the car. They drove him to another part of the camp, then led him to Amr al-Absi, who was standing nearby, pistol in hand. Al-Absi slowly loaded bullets into the gun as Jay was forced to his knees in front of him. Jay thought of his loved ones, his short life, and the pain of the bullet striking his temple.

Without saying a word, al-Absi finished loading the gun and pointed it at Jay's head. As he squeezed the trigger, Jay closed his eyes.

He heard a bang. Jay flinched and gasped but felt nothing. He opened his eyes.

Al-Absi was laughing. The gun had been loaded with blanks. "Did you die, Abu Assya?" he said.

Al-Absi reached out with his hand and touched Jay's neck. "You have soft skin," he said, as if he were going to take it off Jay and make something with it.

Jay was confused and frightened. Was he there to die or not? He watched as a jihadi went to a machete hanging on the wall of a house. "I thought I was going to be beheaded," he said later, "because that is the judgment on the spies."

The jihadi approached and turned the blade of the machete to its flat side. Then he began beating Jay with it. The other fighters joined in. They kicked my son. He tumbled over on the ground. The blows kept falling.

After being beaten senseless, Jay was dragged back to his hilltop prison. He'd failed his second test and knew that he had no chances left. The next time he messed up, he was surely going to end up in a hastily dug grave. The beatings resumed with a new urgency. Every day, his brothers would arrive bearing a new instrument of torture. The latest was electrical cables. When he first saw the cables, Jay thought he was going to be electrocuted, but the jihadis stripped of his shirt and whipped him instead.

They left festering welts on his backs and legs. The pain was excruciating.

Jay sat in his cell and thought about how he'd gotten to this place. Was there any end to this nightmare? *I've done nothing wrong,* he thought, *but these men want to kill me.* He could no longer walk. The pain from the beatings and the deep bruises on his legs and torso made it too painful.

Outside Jay's cell, momentous things were happening. Abu Bakr al-Baghdadi, an Iraqi jihadist who'd emerged from an American prison even more radicalized than before, was on the march. He was the leader of the Islamic State, which was conquering mile after mile of territory in Iraq. To understand where he came from, and how it affected Jay, it's important to look back a bit.

ISIS really began in Iraq. Its roots lie in the Sunni Salafist group known as al Qaeda in Iraq, which was founded under a different name in 1999 by the Jordanian Abu Musab al-Zarqawi. Al-Zarqawi had been a radical—really a revolutionary—for many years. In the '90s, he'd attempted to overthrow the government of Jordan because it wasn't extreme enough for his tastes. When George W. Bush invaded the neighboring country of Iraq, al-Zarqawi saw his golden chance to establish a strict Salafist state and made his way across the border with some fellow fighters. The invasion had left the country in chaos, and the Jordanian and his radical brethren were able to organize without a king or a president breathing down their necks.

Al-Zarqawi allied himself with Osama bin Laden, and his

group of jihadis became the Iraqi affiliate of al Qaeda. He went to war with American soldiers and what was left of the Iraqi Army, specializing in guerilla attacks, IEDs, and suicide bombs. As vicious as he was, al-Zarqawi found support among the country's Sunni tribes, who felt that they'd been shoved out of power after the fall of Saddam Hussein. Young men and ex-soldiers who'd been purged from the ranks of the Iraqi Army flocked to the black banner of al Qaeda. Its aim was to seize control of Iraq and establish extremist Sunni rule.

The U.S. Air Force soon dealt with al-Zarqawi. He was killed in an American air strike in 2006 and was succeeded by the Egyptian Abu Ayyub al-Masri. Al-Masri and his troops went on a tear, gobbling up huge swaths of territory, especially in the Anbar Province, where the Sunni tribes were strong. Wherever ISIS flew, sharia law was put into effect. People convicted of serious offenses were beheaded; those thought to be spies or infiltrators got the sword, too. Minor offenses resulted in the loss of a hand, or a hundred lashes. Women were often confined to their homes unless accompanied by a male relative.

In 2010, Abu Bakr al-Baghdadi was named as the new leader of the Islamic State after al-Masri's death. He was a shy, devout Iraqi who'd been an obscure religious scholar before taking up arms on behalf of a future caliphate. He'd been released from an American prison, where he'd met and bonded with a host of men who would become the leadership of ISIS. Al-Baghdadi was nothing if not ambitious: feeling that he was the true leader of the Islamist movement, he cut ties with al Qaeda and declared, in a famous speech given in a mosque to hundreds of his followers, that the time of the caliphate had arrived.

ISIS existed in the middle of a vacuum. The Middle East was changing rapidly. The Arab Spring erupted in 2010 and reached Syria soon after. In the small town of Daraa, a young boy and his friends wrote on a wall a piece of graffiti: "The people want the fall of the regime." This was a popular slogan of the protests that were rolling through the region. President Bashar al-Assad, who many in the West had believed was a mild-mannered type who secretly harbored a desire to modernize and liberalize his nation, now showed his true colors. Fifteen boys were arrested and tortured, and the security forces mocked their families' attempts to save them. The rage that had been building in the Syrian people for many years exploded.

On March 15, 2011, young people in Damascus took to the streets, chanting their demands: for political prisoners to be set free, for Syria to become more democratic and its government more transparent. Assad sent his soldiers and undercover agents onto the streets to crush the protests. They opened fire with live rounds on the young men and women and left several of them dead and wounded.

But the protestors didn't stay in their houses in the days after the killings. The old fear that had ruled their parents and grandparents had subsided somewhat; it seemed that this was the chance for their generation to seize its moment. The young men and women emerged back onto the streets and amped up their protests, even burning down the headquarters of the president's

Ba'ath Party. People began speaking out for the first time in their lives, taking off the protective covering they had worn like heavy overcoats. As two Syrian authors said:

> This is where the revolution happens first, before the guns and the political calculations, before even the demonstrations—in individual hearts, in the form of new thoughts and newly unfettered words. Syria was once known as the "kingdom of silence." In 2011, it burst into speech—not in one voice but in millions . . . Nobody could control it—no party leader or ideological programme, and least of all the repressive apparatus of the state. (From *Burning Country*, Robin Yassin-Kassab and Leila Al-Shami)

I saw this in Syria. I met people who still had tiny traces of that original joy in their voices. They'd rush up and try to tell you how beautiful it had once been, this rebellion.

People began to die on both sides, both police officers and protestors. Assad placed the responsibility for the attacks on agents of foreign governments—he threw in some nonsense about Israel, too—but the Syrian people weren't fooled.

The protests grew larger, their aims expanded. Now they were demanding that Assad himself leave office. By late April 2011, the demonstrations had spread to a host of cities, which prompted Assad to unleash total warfare on his own people: tanks, planes, entire divisions of soldiers were now turned against the rebels. The bloodbath that resulted radicalized many among the protestors. They understood now that they would have to take up arms against the regime if they had any hope of living in freedom.

The country tipped into civil war. Protestors took over police stations and emptied their armories of their rifles and shotguns. Army battalions defected to the other side. In July 2011, a number of Syrian officers denounced the Assad regime and founded the Free Syrian Army. They began organizing the protestors—who represented many different factions in Syrian life—into one rebel force. The FSA had many admirable ideals and was anything but an extremist organization. I met dozens of the young men who'd been with it from the beginning and I found in them some of the same ideals I would have been happy to fight for: freedom, justice, an end to corruption.

Even from the beginning, though, the opposition was hobbled by the motley crew it tried to lead. There were secularists, Islamists, Communists, exiles, and jihadis all mashed into one "army." It was doubtful if it could have held together long enough to defeat Assad, let alone to give the country a government. But, at least in the beginning, it was a noble venture.

By the late summer of that year, the Syrian Civil War was fully under way. The government saw in the rebels a threat to their existence, and many of Assad's supporters—Christians, Shiites, and members of Assad's Alawite sect especially—agreed. They believed that, if the FSA won, the militants among them would eventually rule Syria and turn it into a theocracy, where their lives would be, essentially, over. There were too many examples in recent history—Iran, Afghanistan—to ignore. And so they fought, right from the beginning, with a brutality that sickened all right-thinking people.

One of the turning points of the war, one that would later influence Jay's life, occurred in 2011. Assad, who was sly like a fox, decided to take the protestors at their words and free hundreds of political prisoners. But he chose them carefully. He released those who were devoted to the extremist cause, and kept the more sane, secular captives in their cells. This way, he could be the hero of his own prophecy: He'd already declared that the rebellion was controlled by radicals. Now he made it come true.

The West looked on in horror at another civil war with the potential to destabilize a major Arab country. What do you do? This time, the answer was mostly *Nothing*, or *Just enough for us to sleep at night, maybe.* There were reports that the British and French sent in special forces to train the FSA, and the Americans provided radios and intelligence information. Which was fine. Great. But there were to be no troops, no planes, no tanks sent to the FSA. It was really like sending cups of water to put out an inferno.

Muslims around the world—people like my son and his brothers—took notice. If Syria was one of the more stomach-churning wars of recent times, it was also one of the most videotaped. The same kinds of atrocities happened in Bosnia and Sarajevo, in World Wars I and II, in Napoleon's invasion of Russia . . . go back in time and read the descriptions of the cruelties of wars, especially civil wars. They will appall you. But reading dusty old accounts and actually seeing people die are two different things. Syria was not only turning into a war that might last for years, it was also shaping up to be an open wound on the conscience of all Muslims. A conflict that would not only draw jihadis to it, but also create them.

Al-Baghdadi saw opportunity in Syria. He sent men and arms into the war zone. These fighters began to establish their training camps and draw rebels away from established groups to fight under their banner. Many of the young men al-Baghdadi sent over the border had been fighting complex guerrilla campaigns in Iraq for years and had become sophisticated battlefield tacticians. They were good, and they were merciless. In 2012, these fighters sent by al-Baghdadi named themselves Jabhat al-Nusra. The group quickly became one of the more dominant forces on the battlefield.

In 2013, al-Baghdadi's organization was renamed the Islamic State of Iraq and Greater Syria, or ISIS. Al-Baghdadi also announced that the Jabhat al-Nusra, which he had basically created and financed from afar, was joining his movement. The leaders of al-Nusra were taken aback; they hadn't sworn allegiance to al-Baghdadi. Their aims were different. Al-Nusra had absorbed some of the local color of Syria; their main aim was to unseat Assad. But ISIS was intent on establishing the caliphate in the lands it had carved out in Syria. The two missions didn't always mesh very well. This was the reason for the brutal infighting between the two groups, some of which Jay would witness himself.

ISIS was on the rise, but al-Nusra and al Qaeda were battling to stay relevant. The truth was that there could only be one global leader in the jihadist movement, and each group wanted the title. With it came legitimacy, resources, and recruits. Rich individuals in Qatar and the United Arab Emirates would back the stronger horse, and teenagers in Sacramento and Brussels and Paris would watch the Internet to see who was inflicting the most damage on the infidels. That was key. In the language of the jihadists, cruelty carried the most weight. The organizations battled to see who could be more bloodthirsty, who could stage the most spectacular bombings. Horrifying to us. But it was like the Cold War, in a way. When global domination is your aim, who cares about a few headless bodies or a few massacred shoppers?

In this race to the bottom, ISIS won. It was simply more creative in its killings, and it didn't give a damn whom it murdered. If you were a Muslim caught up in a suicide bombing, you were acceptable collateral damage. If you were a Christian, you deserved it. If you were a Yazidi, Allah ordained your death. As one journalist wrote, it was like a bidding contest at an auction and ISIS was the rich dude who wanted that Picasso painting more than anyone else. It won the auction, and it carried the trophies away: more money, more men, more Islamic realness.

At one point, later in the battle, al Qaeda got fed up. It released a statement condemning ISIS violence.

The method of destruction, sowing and stirring dissension and corruptions, confusing efforts, making *takfir* [branding

as an infidel] upon those who disagree with them, then this is
a method of a feeble and failed person who has no perfection
except ruin . . . Muslims opposed to ISIS are being tricked
by the fatwas of the donkeys and the mules of knowledge.

It was useless. Al Qaeda only made themselves look like a bunch
of doddering old fools, bitching about how the young hipsters
were ruining everything with their newfangled way of killing
people. If you looked at it from a certain angle, it was almost
funny that the people who murdered almost three thousand
people on 9-11 were complaining about ISIS being *too cruel.*

Today, I don't really care which of these animals wins the
door prize. I can only hope they kill each other off as quickly as
possible.

But, the battle between the jihadists made Jay's situation
more dangerous than it needed to be. This was because Amr
al-Absi, the head of Jay's fighting group, the Mujahideen Shura
Council, was entranced by ISIS's declaration that it was entering Syria. He saw the writing on the wall; he was smart that way.
As soon as al-Baghdadi announced that the group was moving
into Syria, and around the time Jay made his way to the camp
in Kafr Hamra, al-Absi contacted the ISIS leadership and
pledged his undying loyalty and that of his fighters to the new
group. Some sources even claimed that the Mujahideen Shura
Council was "the first branch for Baghdadi in Syria." Abu Bakr
al-Baghdadi named al-Absi "the Wali of Aleppo," which meant
he would be the point man for ISIS in the area.

Jay had chosen the wrong army to join.

The political and military landscape around Jay's prison had changed without him even lifting a finger. He knew nothing about what was happening outside the walls of his jail, but the new realities meant that, while he was sitting in prison, Jay had "joined" ISIS. He'd had no choice in the matter. This also meant that his situation, already grim, had gotten even darker. Compared to ISIS, the Mujahideen Shura Council was a bunch of goofy dilettantes.

Chapter Eleven

IN AUGUST, SOME FIGHTERS CAME and took Jay out of his jail cell. "I was told that I had to appear in a court," Jay remembered, "and afterward, I would be freed." His spirits rose. Even if this was a sharia court, he would have a chance to gain his liberty. After weeks of feeling like an outcast, it was a shot at redemption.

His fellow jihadis tied his hands and blindfolded him. They put him in a car and drove him to a strange room in Aleppo, over the same road I'd taken months before. It was a court led by a Dutch-Moroccan extremist named Abu Ubaida al-Maghribi. Ubaida was young, in his early twenties, tall and thin; he'd studied to be an engineer before leaving to perform jihad. Jay didn't know it, but Abu Ubaida wasn't just the director of the prison; he was the most important security chief for ISIS in the Aleppo area.

Jay's fellow fighters gave evidence: Jay was reluctant to go to the battlefield; he'd tried to escape with the Belgian guy; a strange man claiming to be his father had come to Kafr Hamra looking for him; and then there was the Mossad text. Jay stood up and gave his side of the story, which basically amounted to the fact that he'd had his doubts but was ready to fight with his battalion.

Abu Ubaida listened to the testimony. When his decision came, Jay felt his heart go cold. The judge had decided against Jay, which meant he would remain in prison. A crestfallen Jay was cuffed again and brought to a new cell, where he was locked in alongside a Jordanian man and two Syrian boys.

Inside his cell, the blindfold and handcuffs gone, Jay listened. He heard the sounds of bombs dropping—Aleppo was still a battlefield—but also something closer to home: men screaming, the sound of blows being struck on bodies. Inmates were being whipped and beaten yards from where he sat. His brothers were torturing other Muslims. There was no way around it.

One evening, a fellow jihadi named Zakaria walked into the prison. He pulled his handgun out of its holster and placed the muzzle against Jay's head. "One shot and it's done," he said. Jay swore that he wasn't a spy and, after a moment, Zakaria put the gun away and walked out, leaving my son deeply shaken. Another time, a fighter grabbed Jay by the throat, pushing him onto the bed as if to strangle him. Other members pointed their rifles at him. *I'm going to die,* Jay thought. *Not as a martyr but as a suspected spy.*

Jay closed his eyes. He felt the jihadi's hands release from his throat and the sound of footsteps. When he opened his eyes again, the room was empty.

After four days, guards came for him. They took him out of the cell and brought him to a different prison in the basement of Aleppo's children's hospital. Before he was placed in the room, Abu Ubaida, who was in charge of that particular prison, took Jay aside. The prison director asked Jay to do *dawah,* to preach to the non-Muslim prisoners inside. The Western hostages had converted to Islam five months before, but Ubaida wasn't sure if the conversions were sincere. He wanted to know the truth.

When Jay walked inside, his eyes adjusted to the murky gloom. It was an ordinary room, the walls painted a tan color, and a stone floor tiled with light brown stone. Even the ceiling was a tan color. Scattered around were bare mattresses without bed frames, and a few reed mats. The room was about twenty-six by thirteen feet. He could tell he was in a basement; there was a sash-window on one side that overlooked a solid wall.

Inside, there were other prisoners chained to radiators. They looked skeletal. In the air was the stale odor of sickness. The prisoners ate and slept in the room, which they were only allowed to leave to use the toilet.

These prisoners were different. Through the dirt on their faces and their unkempt beards, Jay could see that they were Westerners. One was the American journalist James Foley and another was John Cantlie, a British war photographer and correspondent. "They were thin," Jay said later. "They didn't get any food."

Foley was a freelance war correspondent who'd been working in northwestern Syria when he was captured in November 2012. He was, like my son, an idealist. Before going into journalism, he'd joined Teach for America and then went to work for US-AID, which distributes humanitarian aid around the world. He was courageous, almost recklessly so: He'd been captured once before, in Libya in the spring of 2011, along with other journalists. One of those men, photographer Anton Hammerl, was shot to death during the incident. Pro-Qaddafi soldiers took Foley and his peers prisoners and beat and tortured them. He spent forty-four days in prison before being released. If the Libyans thought that the experience would make him gun-shy, they were wrong. Foley soon flew back to Libya and reported on the capture of Muammar el-Qaddafi.

After Iraq, Foley went to Syria and reported for Agence France-Presse and GlobalPost, while also working on a film with John Cantlie. Cantlie was a survivor of kidnapping as well; he'd undergone a terrible experience during a border crossing from Turkey into Syria in July 2012. After being taken, Cantlie and another photographer attempted to escape—he said later that it was "every Englishman's duty" to try and free himself—and were shot in the process. A bullet hit Cantlie in the arm and deadened a nerve there, leaving his hand badly injured and only partially usable afterward. The escape attempt failed and the pair were told they would soon be killed. But a week later, fighters from the Free Syrian Army stormed the camp where they were being held and rescued both men. After recovering from his wounds, Cantlie—like Foley—had gone back to the war zone.

Before the pair were captured together, Syria had become the most dangerous place in the world for journalists. But Foley was drawn to the front lines; he felt that someone had to tell the world what was happening there. "That's why I came to Syria," he said at the time, "and it's why I like being here now, right now, right in the middle of a brutal and still uncertain civil war. Every person in this country fighting for their freedom wakes up every day and goes to sleep every night with the knowledge that death could visit them at any moment. They accept that reality as the price of freedom. . . . They're alive in a way that almost no American today even knows how to be."

Foley was alive in that way. He was compassionate and brave. He also knew where he was and what that meant for a journalist. "I don't want to get murdered in Syria," he wrote to a friend. But he continued to do his job. He and Cantlie were at an Internet café in the province of Idlib on November 22, 2012, using the computers to check their e-mail. Unbeknownst to them, their presence had been noticed and when they left the café in a taxi, they were followed by a Hyundai van. Several miles away, in a deserted area between checkpoints, the Hyundai sped up and forced their car to pull over to the side of the road. Armed figures jumped out of the van and ran up to the car, pointing rifles at the heads of the occupants. There were three gunmen. They took Foley and Cantlie and left their translator and the taxi driver. The men had been kidnapped—Foley believed by Jabhat al-Nusra—and had ended up in the basement prison.

Foley was in desperate shape. Because he was an American, the captors were very severe. They'd beaten Foley mercilessly and even waterboarded him. After the group swore allegiance to ISIS, the brutality increased. Jay studied James's emaciated body.

The bones of his face stuck out. Jay noticed freshly healed scars on James's ankles. Foley told him that guards had chained his ankles to a metal bar, which was hung from the ceiling, for hours at a time. Guards regularly marched him outside for mock executions.

Negotiations between the American's captors and his employers at GlobalPost had been under way for months but no agreement had been reached. The kidnappers had initially demanded 100 million euros (or about $130 million U.S. dollars), a crazy amount. Foley was a valuable hostage. His captors moved him often to keep his location secret. And now Jay was ten feet away from him.

They began to speak. "We exchanged our contact details and promised each other to meet again, once we would be free." Jay wrote the names of James's mother and John's wife in a booklet he carried with him, so that he would know who to reach out to if he won his freedom.

There wasn't much to do in the prison. Occasionally, shots rang out; ISIS preferred bullets to beheadings, for some reason. Or one of the Westerners would be taken out to be tortured, returning with his face and his clothes bloody. It was almost a ritual.

To while away the hours, Jay and the other two prisoners started playing word association games. Since the Westerners were chained up, it was all they could think of to do. One of them was "Animal, Mineral, Vegetable." One of the prisoners would think of an object that fell into one of those categories. They would say, "Animal," and the others would start asking questions. "Does it have horns?" "Can I play with it?" The questioners had twenty chances to gain clues before they had to make a guess.

It was a kid's game. In that little dungeon, these war-weary young men returned to being boys.

The days went by. Slowly, James became a kind of father figure to Jay, offering him advice. He was incredibly strong in spirit, a selfless person who lived his beliefs, no matter the cost. He and Cantlie began to speak to Jay about Islam. "They told me they weren't living really good lives before," Jay said later. "They didn't respect their mothers enough, for example." Five months after their capture, they'd converted to Islam, inspired, no doubt, by a hope that it would make their captors see them as fully human. Now they prayed together with Jay for a return to freedom and their loved ones.

Chapter Twelve

AFTER I LEFT SYRIA, I met members of a charity called "Time4Life." They were assembling medicines to bring into Syria, where the health situation was increasingly desperate. I told them I wanted to help, that I had connections in Syria and would bring their medicines to clinics and hospitals near the front lines. They were happy to have me. In May, I reentered Syria, legally this time.

Time4Life's plan was to drop off a load of toys and medicines in a refugee camp in Azaz, twenty miles north-northwest of Aleppo. That was terrific, but I told them I could get some of the supplies closer to where they were needed. They gave me boxes of medicine and said, "Godspeed." I called up some of the activists I'd met on my first trip and told them what I had. It was a chance to return the favor they'd done me, and to meet some real players who might lead me to Jay.

One of my contacts introduced me to an emir from Jabhat al-Nusra. I also met my first Belgian fighter, a man named

Abu Faris. He was originally from Brussels and confirmed for me that my son was in Syria and doing OK. I was overjoyed to hear it.

"I will negotiate with his emir, try and get him back," he said. I had so many questions for him. I even put him on the phone with Helen, who asked the things a mother asks: *Does he have enough food? How is his health? How is he feeling about returning home?* Unfortunately, we had no answers for those questions.

Whenever I dropped off a supply of medicines, I would seek out the leader and ask, "Have you seen any Belgians?" I was more than just a father now; I was a man with connections in the West, someone who could get things done. I tried to use that influence. But no one had seen Jay. No one had heard of him. It was as if he'd been atomized into thin air.

While in Aleppo, I met a Syrian named Abu Harb. He was a big man, fearless. He was one of the Free Lawyers of Aleppo. In the chaos that was that city, a group of men and women had come together to keep some kind of justice alive. The new "judges" that had been installed in the courts often had no legal background; they might be imams or civilians who'd had one or two weeks of training and then been put in the judge's seat. Each court became a fiefdom belonging to whichever fighting group controlled that area.

The Free Lawyers decided to fight back. They came together to try and create a judiciary that was free and fair. When Abu Harb heard of my mission, he came to me and said, *What if we used the courts to try and get back your son?* To me, it was wonderful and crazy at the same time. Who listened to a court in a time of civil war? But Abu Harb wanted to try.

We went to the civil court in downtown Aleppo. When we walked in, we could have been in Antwerp: it was a modern office with computers and secretaries typing away on keyboards. I marveled at the ability of the Syrian people to keep some semblance of civilization running in the midst of the war.

There were two main courts in Aleppo: the civil, "liberal" court and the Salafist court. Abu Harb explained to me that the latter was dangerous to try: The judges ruled on the basis of sharia law, and their judgments are often immediate. If they ruled against you, you could be dragged off to jail that very moment. Or even taken out to be shot. A suspected thief who went before the civil court could be judged innocent because of lack of evidence, while the same man in a sharia court could have his hand cut off half an hour after deliberations began.

Abu Harb wanted to try both courts. The sharia court, I couldn't even enter. Without a beard, and with my fair skin, I would have instantly prejudiced the case against my son. Abu Harb started calling his friends while I went out to the streets, searching for one good clue on Jay's whereabouts.

I had some bad moments with Abu Harb. I was in Aleppo traveling back from a meeting with fighters when we heard bombs detonate three blocks over. I looked up. Far up in the sky, just above a billowing mushroom cloud of smoke, so high you could barely make it out, was the tiny glint of an airplane.

"What's going to happen?" I asked Abu Harb.

"Only Allah knows," he said.

Then I heard it. A thin *AAAAIiiiieeeeeeeEEEEEEEE* sound, getting louder. It was a bomb coming down, but I had no way to tell where it would hit. As I looked around for somewhere to hide, there was a big explosion and the windows in the nearby shops shattered. I ducked down, my ears popping from the concussion. When I looked up, white dust was rising from the ground and the sun was glinting off shards of broken glass.

I looked at Abu Harb. His normally tan skin looked white as alabaster.

"Close," he said.

One evening, after we're returned from another fruitless search for my son, we were sitting in one of the apartments the lawyers used. I felt discouraged; the judges at the civil court told us they had no jurisdiction to try and find Jay and get him back, and the sharia court said any action could take six months. I'd been naïve enough to believe that once I entered Syria for the second time, I would find Jay within a few days. Now I saw nothing but obstacles.

I told Abu Harb and the others that I'd like to pray. But I didn't want to use a Christian prayer; I was surrounded by Muslims. Instead, we all held hands and stood in a circle. I was looking for the right words to say when suddenly an old song popped into my head. "We Shall Overcome." I began to sing it.

I thought of Jay as a boy, of his love for the dinosaurs he wouldn't allow to fight, and of Pinocchio, and his little voice chirping for me to play Harry Belafonte. Of how he looked then and how innocent he was. I started to cry. I felt as though there was danger all around, and that I was alone in this strange world. I feared I would find that Jay had been killed and I would have to see his body torn up by shrapnel or bullets. "Oh, deep in my heart," I sang, "I do believe, we shall overcome someday."

With that song, I was making my peace with the possibility of dying or of knowing that Jay had passed. No matter what happened, I'd come to Syria with love in my heart.

Why did I choose "Overcome"? I can't say that I did. It just came to me. I'd seen documentaries on the Civil Rights Movement in America and I knew the history of the song. I'd been so moved by how people, knowing they were about to be beaten and dehumanized, would gather together, hold hands, and begin singing. It was as if they were reminding themselves they were divine creatures and their cause was worthy.

The song reminded me of home, in an odd way. I felt like my government had abandoned me, and that I was in danger, but that nothing would stop me from finding Jay.

I looked around and I couldn't believe it. A few of the Syrians were singing, too. They even knew the words!

I felt it was a sign—from whom, I didn't know.

One day, I went to meet some activists in an area called Al-Shaar, near one of the courts that Abu Harb had told me about. The street we were going to was in flux. The more liberal Free Syrian Army shared control of it with the more conservative al-Nusra. But one of my sources had told me that I should go there, that there were some foreign fighters who might have met my son. Plus, there was a television station there that wanted to interview me for a story. Maybe someone who was with him would see it; maybe even Jay.

To get to the meeting, we had to cross into eastern Aleppo, the rebel stronghold. Western Aleppo was like a normal city, with clean streets, taxis, dentist offices, and shops open for business. But the closer you got to the east, the clearer the signs of war were. Collapsed buildings, bullet holes in cement walls. I looked up and spotted helicopters dropping barrel bombs farther out over the eastern sector. Barely visible or audible, just a speck of black and a thin buzz.

The east/west border of the city was a sniper's alley. There were gunmen high up in the apartment buildings looking for targets, many of them shooting from holes punched in apartment walls. There were signs hung near the alley: BEWARE—SNIPERS! When we got close to it, I saw civilians afraid to cross over yelling across to friends or loved ones on the other side. They were having entire conversations across the wide lane; it was like the division between East and West Berlin during the Cold War. There was no wall, just a dividing line ruled by invisible gunmen.

We had to wait for our guides to tell us it was clear. After three dashes from one building to another to get a better vantage point, I was gasping for air. *These goddamn cigarettes,* I said to myself. *They're going to kill me before I even get shot.* I thought that I'd been in decent shape. But there is normal-life shape and war-zone shape. I didn't qualify for the latter.

We crossed early in the morning and made it without getting killed.

Western Aleppo felt modern to me; it could have been a city in Europe. Eastern Aleppo was another place. It was filled with historic districts, with narrow arched alleyways built in the twelfth century. You could hear the rumble of generators from inside ancient sand-colored buildings; the electricity was often cut off in the East.

We were scheduled to meet with some activists. When we found them, Abu Harb introduced me and I told them what I was trying to do. A petite young blond woman named Sabine came up to me. She was devoted to getting humanitarian help for people in the city; that day, she was in eastern Aleppo working with a charity that empowered women. I was startled to see her. She was dressed in a T-shirt and jeans, just like a young woman in the West. Across her neck and shoulders was a scarf, but she was unveiled. That was rare in conservative eastern Aleppo; even I knew that. This was a brave woman.

I walked over to her and shook her hand. "You're the first normal woman I've met in Syria," I said to her.

She laughed. "What do you mean?"

"You shook my hand."

Sabine made a face. "You haven't seen the normal Syria yet. You've only seen the bearded guys. I'll take you around to see the real Syria, if you like."

By late afternoon, it was time to cross sniper's alley back to western Aleppo. I asked to go with Sabine; her courage gave me courage. "Dimitri," she said, "you don't understand. I have a lot of security problems. I'm Kurdish, I'm female, and I don't wear the hijab. There are parts of Syria where they will see me as a threat. You're not safer with me."

The experience with Joanie had given me a taste of what she was talking about. But Joanie was a journalist, and that gave her a certain cover. Free Syrian Army rebels who wanted to portray their movement in a good light would talk to her. They gave her access. And her Western looks also gave her cover.

But Sabine was a Syrian. She didn't have the protections that Joanie did.

Still, I told her I wanted to go with her. "I feel safe when you're around," I said, smiling. Maybe I was flirting a bit. But just to see a woman's face and have a real conversation was like manna to me; I felt like it was back in normal life.

"OK," Sabine said. Later, she told me how shocked she was that "this huge guy, with muscles, was feeling safe because of me, this teeny tiny creature." But Sabine had a big heart, and she was willing to help anyone she came across.

"Just relax," Abu Harb said as we started walking west. "And if anyone says anything, don't say a word. I'll talk to them." As we walked, Sabine told me she usually crossed over early in the morning, when the snipers were still asleep. Now it was around 5:30 P.M., one of the worst times to pass.

We walked to a building at the borderline that looked out on a wide street. As we stood in one entranceway surveying the border, I heard a rifle report. A tiny chunk of concrete popped out from the building next to me. I flinched, and I felt the blood drain from my face. It was a sniper. He'd missed me by about three feet. I ducked back inside.

We turned back and found an alleyway that led to western Aleppo. Ahead, there was a tall gate that we had to get through to cross over. People were coming back and forth, glancing anxiously up at the surrounding buildings. But I didn't see anyone ducking actual bullets.

As we moved toward the gate, I spotted a young boy with a Kalashnikov. He was about fourteen or fifteen, wearing a djellaba, standing in front of the gate with the gun across his chest, pointed downward, his finger on the trigger. I thought his eyes had locked onto me. In them was an odd, frightening expression. It was wonder and outrage mixed together.

The boy had seen something that enraged him. His body language—it was just hostile. He began shouting something. The barrel of his rifle came up and pointed at us.

I felt my heart jump. I thought it was me he was angry about.

"Who is this kid?" I said to Sabine.

She looked up and spotted the boy.

"His accent is Libyan," Sabine said. "And he's angry with me."

We were thirty feet away from the boy. He was shouting at us in Arabic; the veins in his neck were popping out with the effort. We stopped. Abu Harb slowly motioned with his hands for the boy to calm down, but it was as if he'd seen a monster. His eyes were bugging out.

"Maybe it's your camera," Abu Harb said nervously to Sabine.

"We're close to al-Nusra territory, maybe he doesn't want us shooting here."

What worried me was the rifle. If the boy, in his anger, pulled back on the trigger just a touch, and if the gun was set to semi-automatic, he could hit us all with a spray of bullets. Abu Harb walked forward to talk to the boy. I turned and found Sabine had ducked behind me, trying to hide herself.

"What's he saying?" I said to Sabine.

"He's calling me a *kafir*," she replied, her voice shaking slightly.

"What does that mean?"

"It means I'm unveiled and . . . and that I'm a nonbeliever."

The boy took a couple of steps toward us and raised the gun to sight us down. Abu Harb reached him and put his hand on his shoulder.

Sabine was terrified, her voice shaking. "They won't let me through dressed as I am. They can arrest me under sharia. And he thinks you are foreign intelligence." She was looking around for an escape route.

Abu Harb's voice was calm in the near distance, but the boy kept advancing.

"Come!" someone cried out. "This way."

A gray-haired man to our left was holding open a door into the mall that bordered the sniper's alley. Sabine and I hurried toward it and rushed inside. I felt the target on my chest disappear.

We were in a little room, an alcove of some sort. Sabine stared at me, her eyes wide, but said nothing. After two minutes, Abu

Harb walked in, his face pale. "The boy is wearing an explosive belt. He was getting ready to detonate it. If he comes in here, we must run."

Shit, I thought. *All this over a woman's hair and a man with a pale face?*

We watched the door of the room nervously. "I have to get out of eastern Aleppo before sunset," Sabine said. She was pale, clearly distraught. "I can't stay here overnight."

Abu Harb tried to calm Sabine, saying that they would take care of her. But she insisted on leaving. Finally, Abu Harb took her out of the little room and walked her to a bus station. The last bus to the West would cross in fifteen minutes, but it was frequently a target for snipers. It wasn't a good place to be, sitting in a window without a veil, your profile exposed in the setting sun.

I waited for Abu Harb's return. I kept my eyes on the door of the alcove, expecting the boy to come through at any moment. But it stayed closed until Abu Harb opened it and gestured for me to come out. We reentered the narrow alleyway and hurried past the boy. He glared at me as I passed, but I avoided his eyes.

That day, I was lucky to be a man. Sabine had been the target.

Later, Sabine told me that a man dressed in a red shirt and a scarf around his neck spotted her at the bus stop and volunteered to walk her across. Because he was dressed "in a modern way," she accepted. Expecting to be shot any minute, they hurried across the borderline as the last rays of the sun shot through the windows of Aleppo.

It was just a normal day. But I felt like I'd just walked through a minefield. Who could know what would set off a jihadi? How could you tell who was friend and who was foe?

I called Belgium to let Helen know what was happening. She was very emotional and it was hard to explain what Syria was like. Our conversations often became difficult and a little heated. They followed a pattern:

"Did you find him yet?" Helen would begin as soon as I said hello.

"No, Helen," I would say. "I haven't."

"Why not?!"

"It's not like you walk around a corner and there he is. It's difficult. I'm doing my best."

"Have you gone to the authorities? They must know where he is."

"There are no authorities. Well, there are many authorities. That's the problem. No one keeps track of everyone who enters. There are many battalions, and I have to find the one he's with."

"He could be in a hospital. Have you checked those?"

"Yes, Helen, I have."

It was frustrating. People back in Belgium expected that I could show up in Syria, go to the local police office, and file a missing persons report. It wasn't like that. In many areas, like eastern Aleppo, there weren't any police. The police station had been blown up long ago.

I went to the hospitals to talk to fighters and ask them if they knew where the European battalions were. They were places filled with carnage, and here I heard incredible stories. In one clinic, I talked to one jihadi who had his eye shot out by a bullet, but who refused to stop fighting. Only after the battle ended did he agree to get help. I met another who pulled up his sleeve to show me a row of burns along his arm. Assad's troops had captured him and tortured him with cigarettes, burning his skin.

When I met people from the regime side, they denied that any such torture went on. "But I've seen the cigarette burns," I said. "Oh, these guys are fighting all the time on the front line, going days without sleep," one told me. "When they get tired, they sometimes take out cigarettes and burn themselves to stay awake." I looked at the guy for the hint of a smile. But he was dead serious.

It was hard to believe they were talking about their fellow Muslims. They were all Syrians, born in the same country.

"Assad is a good president, a good man," his loyalists told me. "He's innocent of all these things he's accused of." I could only stare at them.

Finally, on day five, I got a lead. There was a foreign fighter with al-Nusra who fit the description of Jay and was willing, even eager, to talk to me. There was no other information on who he was.

"Could it be him?" I asked Abu Harb.

"I don't know. Let's go talk to him."

We drove to the al-Nusra headquarters, located in a drab villa that needed a fresh coat of paint. I felt my heart racing. Just to touch my son's face, to hear his voice—it seemed like the most precious thing in the world. Once I was with him, I would never let him go.

We entered the living room. A young man who'd been sitting on the ground stood up at my approach. My heart skipped a beat. The boy was mixed race and had a scraggly beard like my son. But it wasn't Jay. Just a young man who looked somewhat like him.

I didn't know what to talk about. My disappointment had robbed me of the desire to get to know this boy. But I was here; I might as well have a conversation.

"Hello," I said. "Where are you from?"

"From Canada." He was smiling. He was only about eighteen years old, with long black hair and a friendly smile.

"How did you come to Syria?'

"It was my dream to come. I finished high school and a month later I was here. Nothing could stop me."

I felt sad for the boy's parents. Did they even know he was alive?

"Do you miss home?"

"No, " he said. "I chose Allah. He is my home now."

Was this a foreshadowing of my meeting with Jay? Would I find him, only to have him tell me that he wanted to stay? I wasn't sure I could take that.

There was nothing else to say. I asked the young man about

his weapon and he brought it up proudly to show to me. A barely used Kalashnikov.

"Where do you get your weapons?"

"When we kill the regime soldiers, we take their rifles. And the Saudis help us, too."

He would soon have a chance to use it. I wonder now what happened to that eager Canadian boy. Most likely, he's dead.

The Free Lawyers of Aleppo became my constant guides. I ate with them, I scoured the city for clues with them, I slept with them. They were my age and older. They had a double purpose in taking me around: they wanted to help me find Jay, but they were also documenting war crimes. While I asked about my son, they would be talking to the emirs, asking about any evidence of government abuse they came across. Did you find torture cells when you took over a building? Did you meet civilians who told you of husbands or sons who disappeared and never returned? They were also searching for any evidence of war crimes, especially chemical weapons. I was proud to be with them.

They were braver than I was, that's for sure. They never took up weapons. They were like people from another time, who still believed in due process and antiquated ideas like that.

The nights were the worst. During the day, I was out in the streets, doing something. I had faith that I would soon meet the right person who would take me to the right villa, and Jay would be waiting there. But at night, I had time to think, and doubts seeped into my mind. I knew that many of the foreign fighters became suicide bombers. What if Jay had volunteered for this?

Couldn't happen, I said to myself. He has love in his heart. He loves life. He loves women. Look at all the girlfriends he had growing up! Most of the suicide bombers, I'd come to believe, were cut off from life. They had no loving connections with their families or women. I'd been told that some of their parents even suspected they were gay and that this drove them to sacrifice themselves. I had no idea if this was true, but I grasped at any justification for believing Jay was alive. My son wasn't someone who hated his own existence. This gave me hope.

But day after day, I got the same responses. "The Belgians are in Kafr Hamra." No other place came up as regularly. All signs were pointing toward the walled villa of Amr al-Absi. I began to believe the emir was lying to me when he said there were no Belgians in his battalion.

But why?

I soon grew convinced that al-Absi had lied to me and that Jay was with his battalion, hidden away. What could I do from the outside to get him to admit that my son was there? I couldn't go back there, that I knew.

I had to put pressure on al-Absi, to drive him crazy with the name of my son. So I began seeking out Arab journalists and talking to them about Jay and my belief that he was at Kafr Hamra, I gave interviews to Arab television stations. I sent emissaries to al-Absi to try and convince him to let my son go. Any emir or leader of a fighting group that I met, I asked them to text or call al-Absi and say, "What is going on with this Belgian?"

I wanted al-Absi to know he couldn't disappear my son without consequences. Jay's name was now attached to his. If he harmed him, there would be consequences. I wanted al-Absi to hear my son's names in his dreams, until he finally said, "What the hell is it with this crazy Belgian father? Let the boy go."

I began to sketch out a plan. Perhaps the problem was my white skin. I asked an Arab journalist that I'd become friendly with, I will call him Faraj, to go to Kafr Hamra for me and see if he could find out something more. Ironically, I was becoming a kind of spy, the very thing that al-Absi had accused me of. But I didn't work for anyone except my own family.

Faraj went. He called me after he'd returned to Aleppo.

"What did he say?"

"He denied that your son is with them," Faraj said. "But he wanted to talk about something else. He's very angry with you."

That knocked me back. "Angry with me? About what?"

"He told me you've been saying bad things about him and ISIS in the press, that they tortured you."

"But they did!"

"They don't consider this torture. They told me they punished you for visiting them without permission and then questioned you for a few hours."

I laughed. "Yes, they did ask me questions. While beating me."

Faraj wasn't laughing. "Amr al-Absi is very angry with you, Dimitri. He said he wants to 'catch you' again."

I told him I wasn't going to let that happen.

"That would be good," he said.

The door to Kafr Hamra had closed for me forever. And despite the generosity of the fighters and the Free Lawyers of Aleppo, I was running out of money again. I had to return to Belgium. My second trip had been a failure.

How many more chances would I get?

Chapter Thirteen

I RETURNED TO BELGIUM, FEELING despondent. My drinking increased. I'd lost thirty pounds from the stress and was smoking like a chimney. I kept calling Jay's phone and texting him. July passed. Then August. I kept searching the Internet for clues, photos, mentions of Jay's Islamist nickname. There were no new sightings.

By October, Jay had been gone eight months. I hadn't had word from him for most of that time. Having seen what Syria was like, I was starting to lose hope. It was so easy to kill someone there; if an emir or a commander decided you needed to die, it was done. There were no records kept. If you died a hero, your brothers would send out messages and commemorate your death. But if they believed you were a spy, they would bury you in an unmarked grave as a mark of dishonor and never tell anyone what had become of you.

Waiting, waiting, waiting. Depression like a heavy stone wall pressing down on me.

September passed.

Then one day in early October, my phone buzzed. I thought it was one of my Syrian contacts or maybe Helen texting me. But when I picked up the phone, it said there was a Facebook message from "Jay."

"Oh my God," I said aloud.

I looked at it in disbelief. *Hi Dad*, it read. *I've heard you've come to Syria. I can't believe it.*

He was alive. He was talking to me. Those words, I can't tell you how much they meant to me.

Jay, I wrote back. *It's so good to hear from you. Are you safe?*

Yes. I'm impressed, Dad.

I felt a surge of pride.

Jay, you have to get out as soon as possible. President Hollande of France, he's going to attack. He's given the green light to the bombers. Please say you'll leave.

There was a pause.

How is the family?

I told him how I'd waited in a chair in our condo every day for the past few months, looking out the window, waiting for him to walk down the street and ring the bell. Every day. This was true. The next part was not. I told Jay that his sister was sick. I even told him that his girlfriend, the blond one, had become pregnant just after he left. He was going to be a father.

It's impossible, he wrote back.

I'd learned my lesson. I didn't yell at him, I didn't ask him if he knew how much pain he'd caused me and his mother. I never asked him if he was sorry. Only love can change a jihadi's heart, I believed. Not guilt.

After I told him about the family, I repeated that he was in danger and had to leave as soon as possible.

Maybe I will leave now.

I nearly cried out. The words I'd been waiting to hear for months. There they were on my cell phone screen in bright white letters. Jay wanted to come home.

To him, though, I played it cool. *To where?* I wrote.

Turkey. But it's difficult.

I will help you.

Not sure you can.

I will help you, Jay.

I told him about the activists and the emirs I'd met, people who now knew about him and were working to get him home safely. He seemed impressed.

Finally, he said he had to go.

Stay in a safe place, I wrote. *Say nothing to anyone.*

It was time to go get my son.

Jay was out of prison. The director had come to him and given him a choice: he could go back to the walled villa or he could act as a lookout for the Sheikh Najjar industrial complex, ten miles north near Aleppo. Jay chose to be a lookout. He convinced his captors that he was willing to fight for ISIS.

It sounded—at least to me, when I heard about it later—like a decent assignment, but that's because I had no idea what

Sheikh Najjar was actually like. It was a horrific place. The complex had once been the pride of Syria, an economic dynamo that contained mile after mile of factories, grain mills, and chemical plants. But the Syrian war had turned it into a nightmare. "Miles of underground tunnel still lace their way beneath," wrote one journalist about the place, "while men from al Qaeda, Jabhat al-Nusra, Jihad Islamia, the al-Sham Brigade, and remnants of the old 'Free Syrian Army' spent [their time] mining the buildings above ground, hacking lorry-wide passageways between their walls and cutting out sniper's nests in every street and on every floor. What had been one of Syria's newest industrial estates was transformed into a place of death: food stores and grain mills were turned into arms storage depots, their basements into dormitories for the hundreds of rebels who lived there." Many fighters were dying at Sheikh Najjar every month. In fact, it was given the name "the Gates of Heaven" because so many went to their martyrdom on its grounds. The more I learned about it, the more urgent getting Jay out of there became.

At Sheikh Najjar, Jay was assigned a sector to keep watch on. Bombs were falling from Assad's planes and he could hear the shouts of wounded jihadis. At one point, he fired a rocket-launched grenade. If he stayed in Aleppo, he came to believe, he was going to die, if not from Assad's troops, then from American killer drones, which constantly hovered overhead.

Jay began experimenting. There were many more jihadis at the complex than there had been at the training camp or the prison, and only a few of them were familiar with Jay's history.

No one, he sensed, was watching him. He began leaving his position to see how far he could get. He even snuck into Aleppo and used the Internet cafés there.

Perhaps there was an opening here. A way out.

I went online and booked a ticket for Turkey. I went into Jay's room and packed some clothes for him, things from his old life: jeans, sweatshirts, sneakers. I grabbed his passport, which he'd left behind. I left that afternoon. I would make my headquarters in Turkey, and send my contacts across into Syria to pick up Jay. If I was spotted anywhere near my son, it would endanger him; maybe his battalion would believe I was going to try a rescue.

I began going on Google Earth and studying topographical maps of the country. I had to coordinate these maps with the reports from my contacts: *Where are the worst checkpoints? Where is the heaviest fighting going on?*

There were violent battles ongoing in every direction outside Aleppo, but it was particularly bad right where I needed to bring Jay out. The most common route from Aleppo to Turkey was due north, to the border town of Kilis. But that area was convulsed in fighting between ISIS and the more moderate battalions. There was no way I could guide Jay out in that direction.

I looked at the map again. What if I brought him out to the west of Aleppo, where the more moderate fighters were clustered, and then straight across to the small Turkish town of Reyhanli? It was about forty miles.

I knew if I guided him wrong, Jay would be a dead man. The penalty for desertion by an Islamic State jihadi is execution. ISIS would have no mercy.

I decided tentatively on the Reyhanli plan. That city would be my base. It was a small place of about sixty-five thousand people, in Hatay Province. It was notorious for its busy border post, which would provide some cover for us. But it was dangerous, too. Just five months before, a car bomb had exploded in front of the town hall and post office. When citizens had rushed to help the wounded, some of them with limbs blown off, another bomb had exploded. More than 50 people were killed and 141 injured.

All the while I was messaging Jay. One thing he wanted to know especially was what would happen to him once he returned to Belgium.

Dad, will I go to prison? he wrote.

I was torn about what to say. I was desperate to get him home. Kris, my lawyer, had already told me that if Jay returned to Belgium he would most likely spend some time in jail. The public mood was not forgiving. There had to be consequences.

What should I do? He was scared that he would go from Syria to a prison in Antwerp. But I had to get him out of that hellhole.

So I lied to him.

You won't go to jail, I wrote to him. *Just focus on getting out alive and let me handle that.*

I didn't feel good about it, but my mind was laser-focused on the moment I would be holding my son in my arms. Everything after that I put off until another time. *Just give me my son back,* I thought, *and then everything will be bearable.*

I flew out the next day and made it to Reyhanli after a full day of travel. The city was what I imagined a place like Casablanca to be during World War II. A place of full of dubious people with dubious plans: operatives from opposing sides, spies, people looking to get out of Syria, people looking to get in. No one ever identified the forces behind the bombings that had killed so many people there, which was typical for Reyhanli. Everyone's motives in that town were murky.

But this was the kind of place I needed. ISIS would be looking for Jay. I wanted a place in the shadows.

I made it to Reyhanli and checked into the Hotel Ali Ce. If you know the region, you know the Ali Ce. It's a slightly rundown pink-and-yellow building on the main Reyhanli road. It's not plush, it doesn't have all the amenities, and it's almost impossible to make a reservation there. But its rooms and its lobby are where things happen. "From morning till well past midnight," wrote one journalist, "dozens of characters gather around the white plastic tables. FSA fighters and generals, aid workers, activists, journalists, Syrian expatriates and refugees and weapons dealers. Once a sleepy hotel in a sleepy town, the Ali Ce has witnessed it all: tortured prisoners, strategic political meetings, secret weapons deals and scandalous stories." Now, hopefully, it was going to witness one more thing: an escape from ISIS.

I didn't choose the hotel because of the history, but because it was centrally located and well known. If something happened, if Jay became separated from the guides who were smuggling him out, he could say two words to anyone near the border—"Ali Ce"—and they could direct him to the hotel.

But would his alibi be? What reason could he give to the checkpoint guards for traveling toward Reyhanli in the first place? I needed a cover story.

I racked my brains. Finally, I remembered that there was a French charity just over the border in Syria there that I'd worked with before. It would provide a cover for Jay; if he was stopped somewhere at a checkpoint, he might be able to say, "I'm going to the French clinic for treatment."

That would be the cover story. Some kind of internal illness that needed special treatment. ISIS sent its fighters to the border all the time; it even sent them into Turkey. *Perfect.*

To bring him across the border, I needed to get a legal visa for Jay. Without it, he could be stuck in Syria. But how could I ask for a visa without Jay present in the visa office? Would the officials give it to me?

I left my hotel and made my way to the government office responsible for visas. It was in, of all things, a big stadium where I believe soccer was played. Turkish police were standing guard at the front door, and inside it was packed with people trying to get their documents. There were two officials working, a woman and a guy. I stood in line, but when it came my turn to go to the window, I stood aside. I wanted to see which official was more lenient. What I was doing wasn't exactly legal. I needed some wiggle room.

The next person in line was a Chinese man. The male official studied his application and said, "Where is your wife?" The Chinese man said, "She's in the bathroom." The official shrugged and stamped the visa. This was my man.

I went up to him and greeted him effusively. I was quite charming, if I say so myself. Ten minutes later, I left the place with a visa for Jay.

But how to get Jay to the border? I called the charity and asked, "What if I hired an ambulance to take him from Aleppo to Reyhanli?" The charity official said, "If we do that and ISIS finds out about it, they'll blow up the clinic." I would have to find another way.

I called two men I'd met in Syria. One was a "flying doctor"— that is, a physician who went all over Syria, wherever he was needed, with a big backpack filled with his instruments and medicines. He knew all the routes in and out of the country. The other guy was an activist. They came to meet me in the hotel and, over tea, we discussed our options. The doctor was a serious, cultured man, a bit shorter than me with a light brown beard. He had a glass eye from some misadventure that we never talked about. He was quiet and brave. I'd met him on my first trip to Syria, where he was a legend for going places other doctors refused to go and helping the wounded.

We decided the best way to proceed was to coordinate a meeting time and place with Jay, and then have both guys go to Aleppo, get him, and bring him to the border. I handed over Jay's clothes, his passport, and his visa. I texted Jay and told him that our friends would be coming to see him and that they would be in Aleppo the following day. He wrote back: *Good*.

I couldn't ask these men to rescue my child for nothing. I didn't want to offend their pride, but I had one hundred dollars in my hand. In Syria, that was a nice amount of money. I pressed it into the doctor's palm. "I am so grateful. Please take this."

The doctor looked at the money. Then with a quick gesture, he threw it on the floor.

I bent over, picked up the money. I held it up to him. "For expenses only," I said.

"Still no," he said.

I had tears in my eyes. This man barely knew me. And if he was caught helping Jay escape, he would be in very bad, possibly lethal, trouble. To meet a man like this at the other end of the earth . . . it's not something you forget.

"Dimitri, we are proud to be involved in this," the doctor said. "We don't want your money. To bring a father and son together is beautiful."

I was moved. "Inshallah," I said. "Thank you."

Some have asked if I paid a ransom to get Jay out. No, never. Ransoms were for Christians and other infidels; for one of their own, it was death.

We started talking about how to actually work the escape. The ambulance idea was out; the clinic would never go for it. What about putting him in the trunk of a car? We could lay him at the bottom and put other things—blankets, bags of food—over him. But the plan held its own dangers. If the guards at the various checkpoints opened the trunk and found him, it was like an admission of guilt.

I felt the risk was too great. Finally, we decided that the doctor and his assistant would arrange a time. Jay would sneak away from his lookout post and make his way to a rendezvous in Aleppo. There, he would meet my contacts and they would get on the back of a motorcycle driven by the doctor. There were dozens of motorcycles crossing the border every day. It was the best choice we had. If they could make it through the check-points without anyone questioning Jay, they could make it to the border and into Turkey.

The doctor and the activist shook my hand. I hugged them both and wished them Godspeed. They left the hotel; they would cross into Syria in the night. Now the hardest part would begin for me. Waiting.

The next day, I kept myself busy. I went out to the market and bought some of Jay's favorite foods: chicken skewers, burgers. I wanted to be ready when he arrived. I stood on the terrace of my hotel, smoking.

My phone vibrated. *We have him. Leaving A.*

They were leaving Aleppo. Good news. Now to pass the checkpoints.

Another text, this time from Jay. *Dad, when do I see you?*

Soon, I wrote back. *I'll meet you at the bus stop.*

He asked about his sister and his mom. I told them they were fine and dying to see him. He was glad to hear it.

Then: *How many minutes, Dad?*

It reminded me of when Jay was a kid. Children always want to know how long it will be until something happened: *How many sleeps till Christmas? How many hours till Auntie comes?* Sometimes it drives you crazy. But now I was as anxious as he was.

A couple of hours, I wrote. *I'm waiting, son.*

I was too nervous to stay in the hotel room. I needed another smoke. I ran down the stairs and out to the street. We'd arranged a rendezvous, a bus stop just outside the hotel. There were people milling about there, and I could blend in and pretend to be waiting for a bus.

I began striding back and forth. My mind wanted to leap forward to that moment when I first saw Jay. Everything else was a blur of cars, faces, more cars, other faces. Nothing sank in.

It was a strange feeling. All around me were the enemy: ISIS fighters who'd come to Turkey for R & R or for medical treatment. I saw them walking by in their djellabas. Al-Nusra was here, I knew, Turkish intelligence was here. People disappeared off the streets of Reyhanli every week, some by choice, some not. It felt like anything could happen.

I got a text. *We're approaching the border.*

Time doesn't move when you most want it to. I walked up and down the street, pretending to look for the right bus. Inside, I felt like I couldn't get enough oxygen into my lungs. An hour passed, then two.

Where the hell were they? They should have passed the border ages ago. I took a deep breath and tried to calm myself.

All of a sudden, a motorcycle came whipping down the street. Fast. I saw that the man driving it was the doctor. Behind him I saw a shape. There was a passenger.

As he pulled up to me, I saw a young man, burnt by the sun, bearded and thin. I ran to him. It was Jay.

I had so many things in my heart at that moment that I wanted to say. But no words would come out. I held him in my arms like a baby.

Jay wasn't crying. He was trying to be cool like the teenager he was, but his eyes were shining. He was free.

Finally, I found my voice.

"Are you hungry?" I said.

He was. We went up to the room. I had my arm over his shoulder, all the way. I didn't want to let him go. I felt like I had to touch his arm, his shoulder, his hair, to know it was the same little boy I'd played with when he was a child.

It was over. I felt a huge peacefulness overcome me. I wrapped the doctor in a bear hug and squeezed him. "Thank you from the bottom of my heart!" I said. He started to cry, and I followed suit. It was good to cry happy tears for once.

I called my lawyer, Kris, to let him know that Jay was with me and that we would have to think about how to get him back to Belgium. Then I called my ex-wife. "I have him, Helen," I said.

She was crying. I put Jay on the phone with her.

It was one of those moments when your sense of gratitude goes on forever. I'm not a religious person, but in my heart I thanked the universe; I thanked Sabine and Abu Harb and all the activists who'd helped me. Debts like that, you cannot repay.

As we sat on the hotel room eating chicken, we laughed and told stories. Jay hinted at what he'd been through but didn't say much about ISIS. At one point, he got up and went to his backpack and pulled something out. It was a djellaba.

"What's that?" I said.

"It belonged to James," he said sadly.

James Foley. I was startled. The FBI would later test the robe for the American's DNA, which they found. Nobody knew where James Foley was at that moment. The djellaba and Jay's eyewitness testimony would be the first evidence in many months that Foley was still alive.

We left Turkey soon after. I had my son and, ironically, I had a much more positive view of people in Syria than I had before. I felt like I'd seen through to the heart of Islam, the true Islam. There is a saying in Dutch that translates roughly to "Unknown is unloved." Meaning, you don't like what you don't understand. People like Abu Harb and the flying doctor had extended their hand to me and shown me nothing but respect and courage.

I was impressed with the hospitality and the friendliness of the Syrian people, and surprised by their openness. Every race was welcome in Syria, so long as you were Muslim. But even an atheist like me was embraced. There was a harmony in many of the people there, which I know sounds ironic because I've spoken about how divided the populace was. What I mean is person-to-person. When they prayed, they often touched their feet together to form a connection. And you know that, all around the world, other Muslims are doing the same, so there is a kind of circuit. And what flows through that circuit, at its best, is love.

I thought back to the time we sang "We Shall Overcome"

together. I was praying for my lost son, Abu Harb was praying for people he knew, the other Syrians were praying for their loved ones. But we did it in the same spirit.

As the plane lifted off from Istanbul's airport, I knew I was lucky. I'd gotten to leave Syria with my son, and with my body and my spirit intact. I sent my blessings to those who were still fighting for good things in Aleppo and on the other front lines.

Little did I know that more battles awaited.

Chapter Fourteen

WE KNEW THERE WAS GOING to be a firestorm when we returned to Belgium. I couldn't bring Jay home just to feed him to the media and legal onslaught that awaited. He was out of Syria, but Syria was still in him; I could see it in his eyes. So we decided to go to Holland to decompress.

As happy as I was to have my son back, he wasn't the same person that had left Belgium. You could just sense he'd been through something. First of all, he was physically weak. He'd lost about ten pounds. He'd seen torture, death up close. The spark in his brown eyes was dimmed; he seemed more subdued than before.

I booked a small villa in a small town by the Dutch coast. I called Helen and my lawyer, Kris, and told them where we were staying so they could join us. The news hadn't yet gotten out that Jay was free, so they were able to slip out of the country, along with my daughter.

Jay and I reached the villa first and settled in. Within hours, we heard a car pulling up. We walked to the front door and saw Helen and my daughter getting out of a sedan. Helen practically jumped out of the front seat and came running to Jay. She wrapped him in a big hug and rocked him from side to side. As with me, words failed her. She couldn't speak for five or six minutes. She just wanted that human touch, to know that her son was alive and unhurt.

In the next few days, I became a kind of counselor. I wanted to make sure that Jay reentered his normal life at the right pace. I contacted his old girlfriend and asked if she would do a Facebook chat with him. She wrote back, "Of course." I got in touch with his friends from the Jesuit school and did the same. Jay had escaped from people who he had thought cared for him but who'd turned out to be vindictive monsters. He needed to know that there were still people in the world who loved him deeply.

He told me things, some of them moving, some of them quite disturbing. When he was leaving Antwerp on his way to Syria, he said that he'd looked around the subway station and taken a mental picture of it, the train cars, the benches, the people, and then he'd said good-bye to all of it in his mind. It's hard to hear that, not just because he was expecting to die, but because in that moment he never wanted to return. He really wanted to go to paradise. Painful stuff.

Perhaps I was bribing him, in a way. *Do you see that your old life contained good things? That there is meaning and happiness outside of jihad?*

One of the best moments came a week after we arrived in Holland. I found a service that allowed you to go horseback riding for an hour at a time and I booked a slot for us. Jay had always loved horses. We spent a couple of hours riding near the seaside. The air was fresh and tasted a bit of salt. It was wonderful; it brought back memories of his childhood, when there were no dark clouds on the horizon.

Jay was still a Muslim, maybe even still a radical Muslim in some ways. He still prayed five times a day, ate halal food, and checked the Internet for news of Syria. I feared that his old friends would come around, or new friends with the same beliefs, and try to snatch him back. Once you're a member of the radical brotherhood, I'd learned, you're always a member. I had to be on guard.

I tried to talk to him about what he was thinking. He asked me to watch some videos on YouTube, and I said, "Why not?" They were battlefield scenes. Even though he'd seen the real situation on the ground in Aleppo, he still wanted to believe that there was a good fight to be fought in Syria. And, in a way, I think he wanted me to be proud of him.

Which I wasn't, to be honest. Fighting for a good cause is honorable. But for ISIS? No, I couldn't be proud of that. But I didn't tell him that.

There was a small, silent war going on in Jay's soul. When he was sitting on the couch, chatting on his phone, or watching TV, or sleeping, I would sometimes watch my son without him being aware. What was he thinking about? Was the poison finally gone?

When your child is young, you begin to realize that they have their own secrets. It might be a friend that they're angry with, it might be a cookie they climbed down the stairs to eat without telling you. It's part of them becoming a person, but when you have that first realization—my child hid something from me—it's always painful. It's more difficult, though, when that secret could kill them. And you have no way into their minds to confront it. You have to trust in the love you gave them years before.

I hadn't been an expert in Syria when I jumped on a plane there. Somehow, it had worked out. And I wasn't an expert in de-radicalization, either. Would I be as lucky with that part of saving Jay?

I asked Helen, "How do we do this? What is the best way to give him a chance?" Some governments were putting foreign soldiers who returned home from ISIS in prison. But I didn't believe that was the right thing for my son. He'd never accepted the brutality of ISIS; he wasn't in danger of trying to recreate that in Belgium. If he was arrested and put in jail for a long time, he would come into contact with the hardest of the hard and his radicalization process would be completed at last. We would lose Jay once and for all.

I asked my lawyer what was likely to happen. "He's going to have to do some time in prison," he said. "The government wants to know all the details of what happened. That's his only leverage. The public doesn't have a lot of sympathy for ex-jihadis. We have to proceed very carefully or he could be put away for a long time."

I knew some cases already of jihadis who came back and went to prison. For them, it was like an honor. They didn't resist it; they refused to give any details about who recruited them or to testify against their former leaders. They wouldn't even co-operate with their own lawyers! Some observers believe that's because they don't recognize the Western system of justice, but I think it goes deeper than that. Prison is a badge of honor. They know one day they will be free, and their status within the Islamic State will be higher than ever because of their incar-ceration.

Eventually, we had to end our little "vacation" and leave Hol-land. I was running out of money, and I wanted to get on with the next part of our lives. Jay had to face his future in Belgium. Those last couple of days by the coast, I felt downhearted. Was I bringing my son back to a prison?

We decided to test the waters. We gave an interview with a Belgian media company, saying that Jay had returned from Syria and that he and his family were taking some time in Holland. Jay denied having been a jihadi in Aleppo. "I worked delivering medical supplies, driving injured and sick people from one place to another," he told reporters. "I love helping people."

Was that the truth? Even I didn't know at that point.

No one came to knock on our door afterward at the Dutch villa; there were no phone calls from Belgian state security. *So, OK, maybe it's not as bad as I thought. Maybe he can just talk to the intelligence agencies once we return, tell them everything he knows, and that will be that.*

We flew back the next day. We had told no one we were

coming back, only Kris, whom I trusted completely. We took a taxi to our condo in Antwerp and holed up inside. Jay was nervous. He had no idea what he was facing.

That night, a Friday evening, we were sitting on the sofa. Jay's old girlfriend, the blond Belgian girl, was with us. We'd just finished having dinner and were watching TV. A normal night, like a thousand other nights in a family's life.

I heard a knock downstairs at the entry door to the condo. I got up. Maybe it was one of Jay's friends or an aunt calling to see how he was doing.

I went to the door and opened it. There were men in suits and casual jackets standing there. Instantly, I thought to myself, *They tapped my phone. How else would they know we'd come home? Or they'd been watching the condo.*

The police asked to see Jay. Upstairs, Helen and Jay heard their voices. They panicked. Jay was terrified—all he could think of was a prison cell like the one in Syria. That claustrophobic feeling of imprisonment seized him. He was having flashbacks to the bunker. Once your freedom has been taken from you, you never forget it.

Helen, too, was distraught. Not knowing what to do, she grabbed Jay and attempted to hide him. Our condo has a small terrace, and the sliding door to it covers only a part of the space; there's a small wall to the right and left as you step out. She hurried Jay out onto the terrace and placed him against the wall. Later, Helen told me his eyes were like an animal whose den has just been discovered. Fearful. Hunted.

Downstairs, I was talking with the security men. I was

astonished at how many the government had sent. At least twenty guys were walking past me, searching the apartment. The officers were polite, I have to say. It wasn't a case of jackbooted thugs kicking down our door or anything like that.

They headed upstairs. I watched in helpless anger. *I just got my son back,* I wanted to say. *Please, let me have him for a while.*

They brought Jay downstairs. I was relieved to see that there were no handcuffs.

"I want to give him some money," I said. I knew he would need it to buy food and soap and things like that. You can even use it to buy TV time. I handed him what I had in my wallet. Helen, too, went looking for cash to give him.

I remember watching Jay being taken out of the condo. It was 8:20 P.M. Odd details stay with you.

Chapter Fifteen

THE POLICE TOOK JAY TO their headquarters and began questioning him. This went on, I later learned, for five or six hours. When he was hungry, they bought him a tuna fish sandwich and a soda. They didn't have him chained to a metal chair under hot lights or anything you'd imagine from the movies. They spoke to him kindly. They agreed with me that he'd fallen into a kind of cult that had used cunning techniques to brainwash him.

The police had a forensic medical examiner look Jay over. What he found backed up my son's story: there were dozens of scars on his stomach, back, wrists, and the tops of his feet. It was clear evidence of the torture he'd experienced in the bunker prison and elsewhere. When I heard about them, I felt a pain deep in my gut. What must he have gone through in that bunker prison, alone, betrayed, whipped like a dog? I wanted to get my hands on Amr al-Absi and the men who'd tortured Jay. It was the same feeling I'd had after being tormented in the villa basement: a desire to demolish the place, to run through it with a tank and crush everyone inside.

Still, he had to show them that he was no longer a member of that cult. It wasn't just a friendly conversation. In the early hours of the next morning, they arrested him and charged him with participating in a terrorist organization.

The only way to avoid a long sentence was to tell everything he knew: about Sharia4Belgium, about escaping to Syria, about Kafr Hamra, everything. Without that testimony, Kris estimated he would get five years in jail. But would he do it?

At home, we sat in the condo. None of us wanted to talk. His sister went to her room. It was devastating. I knew Jay was safe and wasn't being beaten or tortured. I knew he was getting good food and was sleeping on a mattress and even had access to a therapist if he really needed it. You tell yourself, he's safe, he's OK, stop worrying. But it still left me with an empty hole in the middle of my chest. I felt that I'd failed him a little. I'd brought him back to this.

It was exactly the same feeling as losing him the first time. You feel your child is at the mercy of huge forces you have no control over. I was depressed.

After a few days, we had our first chance to visit Jay. Helen, his sister, and I went together. When we were brought into the meeting room, I was relieved to see that Jay wasn't behind glass. He was sitting in a chair. Helen embraced him, and so did I. Then I went down the hall to the vending machines and bought him a Snickers and a Fanta.

He told us he was fine. The prison officials let him exercise and socialize. They even let him use a PlayStation. I could tell that the prison was making an effort not to stigmatize Jay and to make him feel like they were on his side against the monsters of Sharia4Belgium. But Syria had planted a seed of doubt in my mind. What if they were trying to use these things to make him talk, to implicate himself? He'd only been out of Syria a couple of weeks. You don't lose your radical beliefs overnight. They must be pumped out of you like a massive dose of poison.

Perhaps secretly I was worried that Jay would never truly deradicalize. His mind was a foreign country to me. What if he told the interrogators that, yes, sharia should be implemented in Belgium? That gays should be killed? That ISIS was right? Not only would they put him away for much longer but it would mean that his heart was still with the extremists. The good news was that Jay was in therapy. He was treated, basically, as a trauma victim.

The FBI flew two agents to Antwerp and asked Jay to meet with them. He agreed at once. They came to the prison and he described for them everything he knew about James Foley: his state of mind, his words about his kidnapping, even his tattoos. It was the first time an eyewitness had given solid proof that Foley and James Cantlie were still alive. I hope it gave comfort to their families. Jay also drew a diagram of the prison where the two captives were being held.

Later, we found out what had happened to James Foley. The beatings had grown more savage. When Foley was taken out of his prison room, his fellow prisoners began to hope that he would return covered in blood, because it meant that he hadn't been subjected to the drowning torture, which they all feared more than almost anything else. In the later stages of his captivity, Foley received a teacup of food per day; he was starved to the point of death. The prisoners were kept in total darkness.

But Foley was still himself. When winter came and the cell turned brutally cold, James handed his only blanket to a fellow captive. What can you say about such a person? His dignity and kindness shames the men who tormented him.

In June 2014, ISIS released a Dutch photojournalist they'd captured and put in the same prison as James Foley. The man had memorized a message from his friend. It's a heartbreaking letter that could have been written by my son or hundreds of other victims of ISIS.

> *Dear Family and Friends,*
> *I remember going to the Mall with Dad, a very long bike ride with Mom. I remember so many great family times that take me away from this prison. Dreams of family and friends take me away and happiness fills my heart.*
> *I know you are thinking of me and praying for me. And I am so thankful. I feel you all especially when I pray. I pray for you to stay strong and to believe. I really feel I can touch you even in this darkness when I pray.*
> *Eighteen of us have been held together in one cell, which has helped me. We have had each other to have*

*endless long conversations about movies, trivia, sports. We
have played games made up of scraps found in our cell . . .
we have found ways to play checkers, Chess, and Risk . . .
and have had tournaments of competition, spending
some days preparing strategies for the next day's game or
lecture. The games and teaching each other have helped the
time pass. They have been a huge help. We repeat stories
and laugh to break the tension.*

*I have had weak and strong days. We are so grateful
when anyone is freed; but of course, yearn for our own
freedom. We try to encourage each other and share
strength. We are being fed better now and daily. We have
tea, occasional coffee. I have regained most of my weight
lost last year.*

*I think a lot about my brothers and sister. I remember
playing Werewolf in the dark with Michael and so many
other adventures. I think of chasing Mattie and T around
the kitchen counter. It makes me happy to think of them.
If there is any money left in my bank account, I want it to
go to Michael and Matthew. I am so proud of you, Michael, and thankful to you for happy childhood memories,
and to you and Kristie for happy adult ones . . . Jim*

At the time the FBI interviewed Jay, Foley was still in the prison
in the basement of the Aleppo children's eye hospital. I'll never
understand why the Americans didn't take the evidence that
my son had given them and raid that place. What were they
waiting for? When the rescue mission finally did come, in

July 2014, the special operations soldiers who stormed the prison found that Foley had been moved. He was later be-headed, a savage act that was released on video.

Jay was proving to be the "golden witness" in the Sharia4Belgium investigation. He gave the secret police everything they asked for: what "scripts" Belkacem had used to turn him against the West, who was involved, who bought the weapons in Syria, the route that jihadis took to Kafr Hamra. After talking with Jay extensively, the police arrested the remaining members of the group (Belkacem was already in jail for earlier offenses) and assembled the charges into a mega-trial. It would be the first such prosecution in Belgium. And Jay would be the star witness.

As the weeks passed, I began to meet the families of the other victims of Belkacem. Ozana was one of the more memorable; she was a high-spirited Brazilian woman married to a Belgian man. Their son, Brian De Mulder, had been a talented soccer player who'd been obsessed with F. C. Barcelona as a boy. Tall, dark-eyed, and slender, he'd modeled himself on Leo Messi, the Argentine superstar that anchored the Barcelona team. He even wore the number 10 on his jersey. Having started soccer at the age of six, he knew little else. This was going to be his life.

When he was seventeen, Brian's local club ran short of money and was forced to cut some players. Brian was one of them. For him, it was as if the world had ended; he could see nothing else ahead of him. For Jay, the crisis had been a breakup with a girl. For Brian, it was the collapse of his soccer dream.

Up until this time, Brian had always been a committed Christian. When he was on the soccer field, a crucifix bounced underneath his shirt. It had been a gift from Ozana, who was a serious Catholic. The little amulet seemed to have worked: his first seventeen years had been free of trouble. Brian was a good student and a nice kid.

After the announcement that he had been cut from his team, Brian looked around for something to fill the void in his heart. Some Moroccan friends asked him to come over to their house to play. He went, and had a good time. In the following weeks, he went back and began to hear the Moroccans talk about their faith. Eventually, he walked to their mosque and began listening.

Here it was, something big. Bigger than soccer. Bigger than school or girls or hip-hop. Brian leapt headlong into the faith, and changed his name. He was now known as Abu Qasem Brazili.

For Ozana, it was a body blow. She'd looked forward to going to church with Brian for the rest of her life. Still, the Western mind-set is to allow children to explore and find themselves, and so she held her tongue. "She thought it was a phase of a teenager—of puberty," said her daughter, Bruna. "*In six months, it will be over*, she hoped. But it became worse with his age."

The same warning signals that I saw with Jay now appeared with Brian. He grew more devout. He unfriended Facebook friends who he felt were not pious enough. He hung out only with the most devout of his peers. His grades began to drop. He grew angry at his classmates, accusing other Muslim students

A young Jay with the entertainer Danny Ray
(Courtesy of Dimitri Bontinck)

Jay performing *(Courtesy of Dimitri Bontinck)*

My son composing music as a teenager
(Courtesy of Dimitri Bontinck)

In Aleppo with my friend Abu Harb (right) and a
high-ranking sheikh *(Courtesy of Dimitri Bontinck)*

In Iraq with some *peshmerga* soldiers *(Courtesy of Dimitri Bontinck)*

Tanks in the middle of Aleppo weren't an unusual sight.
(Courtesy of Dimitri Bontinck)

Some Syrian friends show me an anti-aircraft gun.
(Courtesy of Dimitri Bontinck)

On top of a Syrian tank in Aleppo *(Courtesy of Dimitri Bontinck)*

Learning to aim a heavy gun
(Courtesy of Dimitri Bontinck)

With a high-ranking "secular" general and another fighter in Kafr Hamra
(Courtesy of Dimitri Bontinck)

With members of Jabhat al-Nusra in Aleppo
(Courtesy of Dimitri Bontinck)

Laura Passoni and her family after their rescue from ISIS
(Courtesy of Dimitri Bontinck)

With a rebel fighter in the basement of an Aleppo hospital.
My nervous expression is due to the armed bomb belt
around his waist. *(Courtesy of Dimitri Bontinck)*

Jay's ID card shown on a jihadi website. ISIS taunted
me by daring me to come get it back.
(Courtesy of Dimitri Bontinck)

The jihadi in the middle threatened me with death after Jay's rescue. He was later killed in Syria. *(Courtesy of Dimitri Bontinck)*

Back home *(Courtesy of Dany Peleman)*

of lack of faith and piety. But he was still Ozana's son. "He was explaining what he was believing, but he was still Brian like we knew him," his aunt said. "Smiling, helpful, generous." The family held on to that.

Three months before he was to graduate, he quit school. Islam had become his everything: his social circle, his university, his guiding star. He spent his time learning Arabic and praying. "It was more philosophical back then," his aunt said. "He was asking things, wondering about God. It was more like learning. He was not radical at all." I'm sure there are kids who stop right there, who become good Muslims and never graduate to extremism. But what parents don't realize is that these are teenagers we're talking about, creatures who are extremists in everything: love, music, friendships. They're more vulnerable to taking the next step.

At this crucial moment in his life, Brian discovered Belkacem. Brian went to hear his lectures and was transfixed. His aunt says he went from a kid with "a golden heart" to a "programmed robot" in a matter of months. I couldn't have put it better myself. It was as if the software inside our children's minds had been rewritten.

He quickly became a hardcore Islamist, lashing out at his mother and sisters for not covering their bodies in public and demanding that only halal meat be served at home. Ozana decided to take desperate measures. She changed houses, moving from Antwerp to the rural part of Belgium. But distance did nothing. Brian kept texting and phoning his radical pals.

Sharia4Belgium wouldn't let go. They came to the small

town of Limburg where the family was living, like vampires. He would leave the house in jeans and a sweater and change into Islamic clothes once he was past the town limits. And he began to press his sisters and his mother to convert. If they didn't, he threatened to "drop them like bricks." The family found these words hard to accept. "It's not the Brian brought up by his mother," his aunt said. "Brian was athletic, he was sporty, he was helping everybody. We never saw him like this."

Brian was more open than Jay. He told his family that he intended to travel to Syria and do volunteer work. "I argued with him, saying there were plenty of opportunities here," Ozana said. "He told me he didn't want to because all the people here were infidels." This was rebellion as well as religion, and teenagers who are in this frame of mind will accept no substitutes. They don't want to care for elderly Muslims in Belgium or give out food in a soup kitchen. They want to be on the front lines, to feel the concussion of bombs around them as they fight for their brothers. I'd had the same arguments with Jay.

Brian's mother kept up hope that he would lose interest, that the obsession would fade. But he was slipping away. "I love you, but you will never see me again," he told his sister one day. Soon after, Ozana walked into his room and found Brian wasn't there. "They had taken my son," she said. He'd left behind his house keys and his cell phone.

The family later learned that Brian caught a flight from Düsseldorf, Germany, to Istanbul. From there, he must have crossed into Syria. Brian was now believed to be on the battlefield in the Syrian city of Raqqa. I had my son back but Ozana was forced to wake up every morning and wonder if Brian had survived the night. If he was dying in some shitty hospital or if he was making a martyr's video before strapping on the bomb-maker's vest and heading to a checkpoint.

The family gave everything they had to get him back. Ozana lost her job. Her daughter spent countless hours on the Internet, just as I had, scanning battlefield photos and watching videos on YouTube. It took her weeks to find the first glimpse of her brother. It was a group of fighters who'd taken a break from the war to pray. Their guns lay beside them as they bowed toward Mecca. She saw Brian.

Ozana and her daughter became homeless, shuttling between the houses of friends and family. Terrified of seeing a report of his death, Ozana stopped watching the news. Eventually, she found a place to live with her daughter, but Brian was gone and not coming back.

Three months after he left, Brian did get in touch through Facebook. He told his sister that he had no plans to return home, and that they should convert to Islam, abandon their jobs and homes, and come to Syria. He basically disowned his family. He railed against the brutality of the Assad regime and told his sister that the medical care for noncombatants was not what it should be. When his sister told him he could come home to Belgium and be a voice for the freedom fighters, he didn't answer her. The family celebrated his birthday when he was away, laying out his favorite foods: steak and French fries. Ozana was me if I hadn't found Jay. A shell of a human being.

Chapter Sixteen

PROSECUTORS FILED THEIR CHARGES AGAINST the forty-six members of Sharia4Belgium, including Jay. There was one overarching charge of being part of a terrorist organization, and then some of the defendants also had specific accusations against them, such as threatening politicians. The trial was scheduled to start in September 2014. Jay was released to live with us as he prepared to take the stand. His release was based on certain conditions: He couldn't travel to a foreign country. He couldn't go to a mosque. He couldn't associate with his old mates. And he had to be home every evening at 8:00 P.M.

If you think this was a formality, I can assure you it wasn't. Night after night, a plainclothes policeman would knock on our door and ask to see Jay. The authorities were taking the trial very seriously. I think every policeman in Antwerp eventually showed up at my condo to check on my son. These conditions would continue for six months.

It was ironic. Jay was forced to be home at a certain hour.

But it wasn't my curfew he had to obey. It was the government's! It was almost funny—I had the entire police force of Antwerp there to see that my son obeyed. I didn't need to yell at him or threaten him with grounding. The government played the role of the bad parent. I got off scot-free! The one silver lining to the whole damn mess.

The stress seemed to build a little every day. I knew Jay still felt some loyalty to individuals within Sharia4Belgium; these were his old friends, his brothers. Now he had to face them in court and denounce them for what he had once believed. It was difficult. The threats to his life increased as the trial drew near. "Judas, we are watching you." "You will not make it to the courtroom." There was one Islamist in Antwerp who publicly threatened Jay with bodily harm.

We had police protection as the trial approached. The officers were practically invisible, but sometimes I would spot one of them when I went out for cigarettes or to have a beer at the local bar. I know Jay was afraid. He was an odd figure: He was the victim of terrorism. He was suspected of terrorism. And he was the golden witness against the organizers of terrorism. A strange position to be in, hated by almost everyone.

Jay was giving interviews to the press to help educate people. Some of the mysteries of his own motivation became clearer. "I don't have any hate toward Belgium or America or Belgian citizens or American citizens," he said. "But I have hate toward the deeds of certain countries. For example, we see Guantánamo Bay . . . and we cannot stand and act like it's nothing."

He also tried to clarify why his friends went to Syria. "Every person has his own reason," he said. "For example, one might not feel at home anymore in his home country. The other one might have a criminal life and he's being harassed 24/7. The other one might have family over there."

Jay didn't talk about Syria to me. I believed he'd seen the light in the darkness. What precisely was going on in his mind at any given time was impossible to say.

But after months of depression, I felt like my life had turned around. The European press was treating me like a hero for having gone and risked my life in the land of ISIS. The Belgian press was far tougher on me, but I was happy to know my mission had meaning beyond my own family. It gave hope to others.

I decided to try and use my story for a good cause. I went to high schools to tell teenagers about the dangers of ISIS. It felt good to be doing something proactive. And I began meeting with other parents whose sons had run away to ISIS. We gathered once a month.

The first time I walked into the meeting I was surrounded by men and women, some my age, some older: Christian, Muslim, white, brown. They listened to me tell my story about what the conditions were like in Syria for the Western fighters that were there. I didn't sugarcoat anything; my meeting with the Canadian fighter came back to me, and I knew many of their sons were just like him, committed jihadis.

After I finished, the questions began. A woman held up a

picture of a handsome twenty-year-old man. "This is my son Joseph. Did you see him in Syria?"

I was startled.

"Can I see the picture?" She brought it forward and handed it to me. I studied it.

"I'm afraid not."

The look in her eyes: desolation. I'd been there. "Don't give up hope," I said. "If I could bring my son home, so can you."

Other parents began talking about their pain and their loneliness. "No one will help us," said a red-haired woman. "They believe our sons will return and blow up the country. How can we convince them otherwise?"

It was a tough task. We needed to have successes, young men who returned home and were reintegrated, found jobs, spoke out against hatred. The Belgian public needed to see with their own eyes that it could work. But that would take time and luck.

Then I got my first phone call from a parent. It was the early summer of 2014. They were Belgian and their son had converted to Islam three years before and then run away to Syria.

I went to the town of Menen to meet with the couple. They lived in a nice villa with a swimming pool. The father was a manager at a nursing home; the mother was a nurse. Good, decent, Christian people. And not struggling. Anyone who tells you that jihadis only come from the projects or the streets doesn't know what he's talking about.

As we sat in the living room of their comfortable home, they began to tell me about their boy, Lucas. They'd adopted the child at four years of age from Haiti, and brought him up a

Christian. He had been a wonderful child who'd dreamt of becoming a policeman one day. Later he'd become a metalworker and a champion kickboxer.

Then something called Sharia4Kortrijk had found him. Kortrijk is a small town in Belgium near where Lucas lived. He was searching, along with his best friend, the son of Moroccan immigrants, for a greater meaning in life. They fell into the trap of Sharia4Kortrijk, an offshoot of Sharia4Belgium. It was like a franchise. Soon they would be all over Belgium, then Europe, then the world. Sharia4London, Sharia4Galway, Sharia4Tuscaloosa. It was as if radical Islam had adopted the marketing methods of McDonald's and put one in every town.

A jihadi who'd returned from fighting in Syria found Lucas and his friend Abdelmalek at the local mosque. He began to fill their heads with the usual trash about infidel aggressors and Muslim victims. He was the one who recruited them for jihad.

Pol and his wife never saw anything wrong with their son. They knew he'd become a Muslim. He'd asked for halal food in the home, just like Jay. He'd changed his friends, just like Jay. In fact, the two boys were the same age.

As they talked, I felt a wave of depression sweep over me. I could almost predict the next words out of their mouths. A child of color feeling lost in Belgium, finding strength and discipline in Islam. And then the bastards had corrupted the boy's mind.

Lucas had been gone only one week at this point; his parents' pain was still fresh. Lucas and his friend Abdelmalek were supposed to come home from school that day. When they didn't arrive, the parents of both boys were worried. At 9:00 P.M., they both received a call from Belgian intelligence: *We're sorry to tell you that your sons have left for Syria.*

What did this tell me? That the cases of Jay and the other members of Sharia4Belgium had at least one effect. The secret police were now watching other suspected jihadis. There was no other explanation as to why they knew so soon where the two boys had gone. But if they'd been tracking the boys, why didn't they stop them?

I listened and nodded, not saying much. Lucas's parents needed to talk. It was Jay's story. There is a blueprint for these conversions and radicalizations and 90 percent of the cases follow it almost to the letter.

We had dinner and coffee. Pol was quiet; he was someone who took care of people for a living. The mother was terribly emotional, unable to finish her sentences. "Please believe we had no idea," she said. "Of course," I said. "If you knew, you would have done things completely differently. Don't blame yourself."

I started to make a file on their son. I asked for pictures. The father, who was more controlled, more stoic, brought them out. I asked the boy's height, his weight, even his shoe size, in case we had to buy him clothes to get him out. Does he use Twitter or Facebook? What are the color of his eyes?

When they'd given me all the relevant information, I told them the bad news and the good news—the bad news first, and there was a lot of it: Lucas had gone so recently that it was doubtful that he'd already become disillusioned with ISIS. He was still in the honeymoon period. The Western fighters spent a month in training camp, and before they began it their cell phones and laptops were taken away. So their son was going to be out of touch for at least a month.

"This is what's happening to your son," I said. "He's in a kind of international hostel for jihadis, filled with young Westerners just like himself. He's found a fraternity of young men who think like him. It's as if he just went away to college. He's not thinking about you; he's thinking about how exciting this new life is. He's loving the hardship; it shows he's dedicated. He's not given much time to think for himself. When he's not training, he's listening to lectures, or he's eating with his new friends, or he's cleaning his gun with his new friends. It's just like joining a cult; all your time is accounted for."

I told them not to expect any quick results. Lucas wouldn't begin to see the reality of ISIS for many weeks. As had been the case with my son, the spell over him was at its strongest now.

The first thing was to make contact. Lucas and his parents were texting regularly. That was huge. Sometimes it could take months just to find the kid and get him to talk to the parents. But Lucas refused to talk about what he was doing in Syria. He didn't even want to get on the phone with his mom, who he knew would be emotional. It was almost as if he was staying in touch with his parents as a courtesy. When I read his messages, which were just short factual messages, with no details, I sensed that his heart was in Syria.

The next conversation was always a difficult one. I tried to explain it in terms that people could understand.

"Look," I said. "There's no long-distance solution to this problem. I know you lie awake in bed listening for the doorbell, hoping that your son is going to change his mind and come home on his own. It's not going to happen. That's the movies; this is your life. For you to even have a chance of getting your son back, one of you is going to have to go with me to Syria."

Both of them lost some color in their faces.

"Why do we need to go?" Pol said.

"Because the people need to see you. If I just show up with a picture of your son, the activists and lawyers and fighters who have the information on where he is will not be impressed. Maybe they'll think I'm being paid to get your son back, or they'll think I'm a spy using this photo as an excuse to see some ISIS camps. If you go, that makes it real for them. They need to see the pain in your eyes. Without that, your son is just a face in a sea of faces. They won't care, and they won't lift a finger to find him."

They talked between themselves. They both wanted to go.

"No, none is too few and two is too many. I need one of you."

I have to admit that the mother's nature was a liability. It didn't pay to get hysterical in Syria; people wouldn't respect that.

They decided that Pol was the one. I breathed a sigh of relief. This was good.

I had found software that could trace the location of a cell phone. I found out through that, and through some sources, that the boy was in Raqqa, Syria. That was bad. Raqqa was the headquarters of ISIS, where their control over their new recruits was strongest.

Pol called Lucas and told him he was coming to Syria. "Do not do that," Lucas told him. But the father was insistent. Lucas finally relented, but asked to meet Pol at a safe zone away from Raqqa. We accepted that. It would be better to have him away from the ISIS capitol anyway.

When you're a fighter in ISIS and you want to leave your fighting group for any reason, you have to ask permission from your emir. The new guys don't have IDs; their European documents have been taken from them and their ISIS ones haven't yet been issued. So they're under the control of their leader. Lucas's emir told him no.

There was no appeal. If you tried to argue, you would be punished. One German fighter I'd heard about had his head shaved after asking once too often, so that his comrades could watch him for any signs he was trying to escape. It would have to be Raqqa.

I booked tickets to Kilis in south-central Turkey, near the border with Syria. On the flight, I could tell that Pol was afraid, as he should have been. Going to a country in the midst of a civil war is not to be done lightly, and Syria at the time was one of the most violent places in the world. I tried to talk to him, to give him confidence. I was trying to send the message: *project strength*. Body language means a lot in places like Syria, where people are fighting for their own survival and might not speak your language.

I tried to prepare Pol. I told him to grow his beard so that he would blend in better, and he did. I told him to bring medicine, especially for diarrhea, because you're going to get it. The water in places like Aleppo is often bad. There are no toilets, only holes in the floor.

And I tried to get him ready mentally as well: "You're probably going to see blood. Hospitals are some of the best places for information, so you have to be ready to see injuries, gruesome ones." What it was hard to prepare them for was the horrible state of Syrian clinics. They weren't the clean antiseptic places we know in the West. Especially close to the front lines, they are filled with frazzled doctors, filthy sheets, screaming patients who haven't been given painkillers and fighters with severe wounds in hallways, waiting for treatment that may or may not come. Life is indeed cheap in places like Aleppo.

Chapter Seventeen

WHEN WE FIRST ARRIVED IN Turkey, we considered asking permission to see Lucas through the sharia court. But we were told it could take six months. We started talking to different emirs, asking them to use their influence to get us a meeting.

Pol grew more apprehensive the closer we got to the border. In a town called Azaz, we asked around and met activists who might know where the Dutch fighters were. Pol grew quieter day by day. I knew that he didn't want his voice to shake when he talked. He didn't want to show that he was afraid.

I remembered crossing the border the first time in my search for Jay. It had been a liberating moment for me. I tried to convey the same emotion to Pol. When we crossed over on a hot afternoon, I turned to him. "Pol, how do you feel?" I asked. "You are closer to your son! You're taking action today, and that is a good thing."

It was courageous of Pol just to be here; many people wouldn't have been able to handle the stress. But Pol didn't respond to me. His head was swiveling back and forth, looking at all the bad guys milling around. His anxiety mounted. Whenever we saw guys with balaclavas and AK-47s, he would stop and refuse to go on. "I don't want to meet with those guys," he said at one point. "Believe me, I understand," I said. "I don't want to meet with those guys either. But they are the ones with the information."

Pol's nerves got worse. After a couple of days, he didn't even want to leave our hotel room.

I had the advantage over Pol and the other fathers I helped. I had my military background; when I was in Slovenia and we heard guns firing, it was our job to move toward it. Not to fight, but to find out who was shooting and to control the situation. So I'd learned not to run from the sound of gunfire.

Plus, I'd gotten used to Syria. The shelling no longer bothered me. And the nonstop action of life near a battle zone was now second nature to me. In fact, I found that part of me enjoyed being back. It's that thing that war correspondents experience: the high of battle. It was thrilling to be so close to where world events were unfolding and to play a part, however small, in the action. But when you experience it for the first time, it can be overwhelming.

I got angry at Pol. I admit it. "I'm here with you to find your son," I said. "If you won't go out and talk to the people, what do you expect will happen? This will be a waste of time. Come on, damn it, let's go!"

"I'm really afraid," he said at last.

"I understand. But your son needs you to act like you're not."

Near Aleppo, we were talking to a group of FSA fighters when one of them handed me a Kalashnikov. I checked it out and then went to hand it to Pol. "Take it," I said. The fighters were watching with tentative smiles on their faces. I wanted them to see Pol as one of the boys. It would help.

"No," Pol said. "I'm against weapons. I've never touched a weapon in my life and I don't want to start now."

I felt embarrassed. This was not the time to be prudish about such things.

I tried again but he refused. The fighter took his weapon and he and his friends walked away.

"Pol," I said, trying to control my anger. "We're in a war zone. The FSA is fighting ISIS ten kilometers away from here. What if they're overrun and we have to fight for our lives? Are you going to pick up a weapon?"

He thought about it. "No. I will run away."

I was amazed. *Run where?*

At least we had the link with Lucas. That helped a great deal. I had Pol call him as soon as we crossed the border. "I'm going to tell you what to say," I said.

Pol made the call. His son picked up and they chatted briefly.

"Tell them you and your wife have split up because of all this," I said.

It was a strategy I'd used with Jay. Create incentives for the boy to leave. You have to change the status quo and make him believe that his decision is having terrible consequences.

Pol told him, then listened. He shook his head at me. The boy didn't want to talk about it.

The next conversation, Pol had another stratagem prepared. He told his son that his grandmother was in the hospital because of the stress of his disappearance.

But the son was adamant. He wouldn't go home.

It was a deadlock. Lucas wasn't listening to his parents, to anyone from his old life. But maybe he would to someone from his new life. It's like gang prevention: If the kid won't listen to his dad, call in someone he does follow. Like a gang leader. That's his new hero.

I found two emirs who were willing to go and talk to the sheikh of the young man's fighting group. They came back and told us, "He's still in training. You can't see him yet." No one is ever allowed to see a jihadi who's still in training. You have to wait.

Pol and I decided to leave. There was nothing for us to do until I got word that he was done with his jihadi schooling. Then we could try again.

I had another reason for not hanging around. I'd experienced some unexpected resistance in Syria. A few fighters came up to me and said, "You got your son back. The Muslims helped you, and ISIS didn't kill him. Why do you still speak against us?"

I was shocked. These guys had seen some interviews I'd done in Belgium and they were pissed off. From their point of view, Syrians had bent over backward to help me and I'd repaid them by criticizing ISIS. Those were delicate moments. One al-Nusra guy told me that I needed to talk to the Western media about ISIS and tell them they weren't all bad.

Other fighters who'd met me before said to me, "Dimitri, you said that once you got your son back, you would think about becoming a Muslim. Well?" I refused to lie to them. I said no, I wasn't converting anytime soon.

The discussions got heated. One time, I got sick of all the talk about "Allah's will" and "Allah commands" and said to an al-Nusra jihadi in Aleppo, "Is it Allah's will that Western kids run away from home?"

"Yes, this is a decision of Allah."

"And to keep people in the war who want to go home?"

"It's Allah."

There was no argument. Everything was Allah's will.

We returned in August. We entered Syria illegally, even though we had stamps on our passports that said we'd gone through border control. The stamps were to protect us in case we were caught inside by officials who'd want to know how we got there.

Checkpoints. Meetings. Phone calls. I connected with the two emirs I'd used before and they made some inquiries. "Lucas is now a policeman," they told me. He'd finally been able to fulfill his lifelong ambition, only in the hellhole of Raqqa. It was now possible to visit him.

We asked Lucas to meet him in al-Bab, a town ten minutes from Aleppo. If we could get him there, we could get him out of Syria. Lucas agreed and we headed to al-Bab. We waited for Lucas to show. Nothing. Pol called him and Lucas explained that he'd tried to make the meeting, but he didn't have the right pass to get to al-Bab. He'd gotten as far as the first checkpoint outside Raqqa, but he'd stopped before approaching it. He was terrified that he'd be accused of trying to escape and be executed on the spot.

Pol stared at his phone. Our hopes were dashed. After that, Lucas's messages became stranger and stranger. One day, he wanted to leave Syria, and the next, he was determined to stay.

I found a guy in Raqqa with a motorcycle. He agreed to take Lucas out. But he would still need a pass and Lucas wouldn't go back to his emir to ask again. Others who'd done that had been thrown in prison or beaten.

I racked my brains. I asked myself: How can I get Lucas out without using the roads? I looked at my topographical maps and stewed in the hotel room. And then I had it. *Camels.*

I made some calls. My Syrian contacts barely batted an eyelash. They would see what they could do. One activist finally called me back. There was a man who could get Lucas across the desert on one of the beasts without using the roads that were clogged with checkpoints.

I was so excited. I'd solved the puzzle! Yes, it was a little unconventional, but here was the solution to our problem. I felt like some kind of wizard able to spirit men out of the midst of savages.

Lucas, however, said no. Perhaps we asked on one of his "stay" days. Pol pleaded with him, but it was hopeless. I was pissed; my brainstorm had amounted to nothing.

Another father had joined us by then. I'll tell his story next, but his son was also in Raqqa. I arranged for Pol to go there. ISIS, flush with victory, had an international media center in the city. You go, you register and, in theory you can meet with your son and talk with him. Pol made the journey across the sands of northern Syria, which was infested with rebels and bandits. I stayed near the Turkish border. ISIS was not a fan of mine, as their threats had shown; it wasn't advisable for me to talk to them.

I was proud of Pol. He'd walked in to the lion's den when every nerve ending in his body was signaling either *turn around* or *run*. It's harder than it looks, disobeying your lizard brain. But he'd done it.

When Pol got to Raqqa, problems sprang up immediately. One of the ISIS emirs met with him and began shouting, "You are a spy! How is it possible that you weren't arrested at the checkpoints?" *Damn*. It was a tough question. Pol and my contacts didn't want to reveal the name of the sheikh who'd sat in the front seat to get the guys through the checkpoints, in case this ISIS emir went apeshit over it and hurt the guy. Somehow Pol and my driver, Yusuf, bluffed their way past the question and got the meeting arranged. Finally, Pol was going to see his son.

When the meeting came, Pol was escorted to a room guarded by five or six jihadis wearing masks and bandoliers of bullets across their chests. I'm sure that gave him pause. But he kept on moving.

The next moment is one you can never predict. What will the son's reaction be when, as a fighter, he sees his father for the first time? What buried emotions from childhood will come to the surface without either person anticipating it? It's an encounter with echoes from the past—the time you went to see your boy at summer camp, or the time you went to drop him off at college—but transported into a nightmarish context. Often, the child is embarrassed that you are there. You are part of his old life. He wants to get on with the new. You're a reminder of a time when he was young and weak and without direction. It's an incredibly delicate thing, with guards watching over you, to tell your son that you want him to be your child again, without humiliating him or making him feel like less of a man.

Lucas was pale, which surprised Pol, and skinny. He looked unhealthy. Pol began telling Lucas why he'd come. The family missed him so much, it was terrible. He begged Lucas to come back to Holland. He could still practice Islam and fight for the rights of Muslims around the world, but do it from his home. The government wouldn't arrest him.

Lucas sneered. "Is that what you came for?"

"Of course," Pol told him. Pol didn't argue with his desire to help innocent people, but why not go to Haiti and volunteer there? Jihad was a journey, an honorable journey. This wasn't the only path.

Lucas refused to listen. Not only would he not return to Holland, but he wanted his father and the whole family to convert to Islam, sell their houses, quit their jobs, pull up their roots, and move to Raqqa. Pol was so stunned he could barely comprehend what he was hearing.

Lucas didn't see this as a meeting to get him back to Holland. It was a way to get Pol and the others to Raqqa.

There was no hope. If anything, Lucas was more determined to stay in live in the Islamic State than he had been when he'd arrived. Pol was staring at a complete stranger. . . . I know I've said that before, but I can't emphasize it enough. This is the *precise physical and emotional sensation* you get in such moments. Your son is gone. In his place is a body snatcher.

In the West, we believe that love conquers all. That the love between a child and a parent is stronger than steel. I believed this, too, for years. But I'm sorry to report that it's not true. Pol had risked his life out of love for his dear boy but Lucas didn't give a shit. He just didn't care. He told his father to go home and prepare to emigrate to Iraq. Madness.

I saw Pol a day later. He couldn't believe what had happened. He'd gotten right up to the edge of victory, touched his son and held him in his arms. And then, failure.

Pol's weakness returned. I had to find a clinic in Syria that would take him in. He just shut down. He needed rest.

After he recovered, Pol told me that he'd gone through the meeting over and over in his head, hundreds of times, examining each expression of Lucas's, down to the last raised eyebrow or twitch of the lip. He had a new theory. *Lucas was actually being held against his will.* Well, maybe not against his will, but under duress. The guards with the grenades and the automatic rifles were indications that he was being forced to stay in Syria. Of course he refused to come home—who wouldn't!

It was . . . possible. Just barely. I hadn't been at the meeting, but who knew? But everything I'd learned about ISIS told me that they didn't hold their fighters to stay at the point of a gun. At least, not in the summer of 2014. And Lucas had gone way beyond saying that he didn't want to go back to Holland. He'd insulted his father and suggested that the whole family convert. That wasn't ISIS talking; that was Lucas.

I told Pol not to give up hope. Keep talking to Lucas, keep showing him that you still love him and will stop at nothing to bring him back. Mention birthdays he's missing, family celebrations, old things he did as a kid. Give him images to contrast with the filth and savagery of Raqqa. Let them do their hidden work.

He agreed. He returned to Holland and his wife. His other son, Christopher, wrote Lucas as well. One of Christopher's messages on Facebook read: "Crying every day, sleeping only two hours, walking into your room without your presence, living without your smile. Come back, brother, you'd make my life complete again. Do it for us, come back. Life is nothing without you."

A year later, Pol and his wife received a call. Lucas had strapped an explosive belt to his body and run at an enemy position near Raqqa. He'd died in the suicide attack.

Finis. The end. And there isn't a goddamn thing you can say.

Chapter Eighteen

JAY'S STORY WAS ALL OVER the Belgian media by this time. People began to take sides, many times based on which end of the political spectrum they were on. "Bontinck says he only did humanitarian work," the mayor of Antwerp told journalists, "but there are holes in his story. He needs to be interrogated. I have no interest as a mayor in having icons of Muslim radicalization or jihadis here in my town, recruiting for a holy war or even being a source of new radicalism and maybe even terrorism perpetrated here on our own soil."

Jesus Christ, I thought. Jay was not an "icon" of anything except maybe mixed-up teenagers. He'd never recruited anyone for a holy war or tried to radicalize a single person. I had no problem with him being interrogated; it was the state's duty to get to the bottom of what happened and what his true feelings were about those events. But the mayor was trying to implicate Jay in a secret conspiracy to bomb Belgium into sharia. And it just wasn't true.

People were worried. It became clear in the next months that a lot of young men from the cities and towns of Belgium and Europe were leaving to go fight in Syria and Iraq. In fact, it turned out that little Belgium was contributing more jihadis to the cause per capita than any other Western nation (though later an even smaller country, Trinidad and Tobago—where youths were radicalized by imams trained in Saudi Arabia—took the title away.)

The security services were working flat-out to identify these radicals in our midst. "Every police, detective, and military intelligence officer in the country [is] focused on international jihadi investigations," one Belgian counterterrorism official told a journalist. "We just don't have the people to watch anything else and, frankly, we don't have the infrastructure to properly investigate or monitor hundreds of individuals suspected of terror links, as well as pursue the hundreds of open files and investigations we have."

That was astounding—every single detective in the country was working on these cases! How was that even possible? I completely agreed with keeping our country safe, but I didn't want Jay to get swept up in a kind of mass hysteria about boys like him. I gave interviews to the press, doing my best to counter the growing call for returning fighters to be thrown in jail. "What these youngsters need is love and family around them," I said in one of those articles, "not to stigmatize them and put them in prison."

I'm sure there were people who were furious at me for defending my son. I was called an enabler and a sympathizer by my fellow Belgians. Many people were very happy that Jay was going to jail. They hated him. They saw him as a terrorist, something that, to me, he had never been. Many who call our sons terrorists don't understand the situation. They think emotionally; they don't even want to know the facts. And they make their minds up in a split second.

Even non-Muslims attacked me online, saying I was an attention-seeker or that I'd made up the whole trip to Syria to make money. Their arguments were nonsense, of course. Why would I put myself through such trauma to make a few dollars? And how had I faked the photos of my trip to Syria? The level of their anger surprised me. I had the feeling that most of these people were frustrated in their own lives and resented anyone who did anything out of the ordinary. I pitied them.

I also heard from the other side, and their message was much more frightening.

The hate began as soon as I our story hit the press. On social media and Facebook, messages arrived in my mailbox. "We know you are a secret Belgian agent who used the excuse of his son's journey to Syria to infiltrate the camps of our brothers," a typical message read. "We are going to find you and cut off your head."

One morning, a friend called me and said ISIS itself had threatened me online. I went to the site he'd found. It showed a picture of me standing next to a Salafist fighter. I recognized the guy. I'd met him in Aleppo. There was a caption underneath: "Secret Belgian undercover agent Dimitri Bontinck standing next to a mujahid who doesn't even realize he's standing against a man who is against jihad *fi sabilillah* ('for the sake of Allah'). Huge security vulnerabilities were highlighted with a single photo. The Mujahideen were located and the hideout was compromised by one single Belgian secret agent."

These idiots thought I was going around photographing their secret sites. I was just taking a picture with the guy. In fact, I think he asked *me* for a photo!

"This man was spying on the ranks of the mujahideen at the bequest of the Qatari intelligence services," the bulletin went on. "They record the faces to facilitate identification later on . . . Bontinck is planning to go back to Syria soon."

The website said that fighters should be on the lookout for me and if we crossed paths, they should hunt me down and kill me. How nice.

I didn't lose my shit over these threats. If the people behind them had been true believers, they would have been in Syria like the people I met. *Talk is cheap* was my attitude.

But I did worry about Jay. He was, in extremist eyes, a Judas, a betrayer who had to be eliminated. Jay showed me the messages he was receiving online. *"You are a traitor, and inshallah you will pay the traitor's price"* was a typical one. There were many more, dozens upon dozens, just like it or even worse. If he was allowed to live, then other jihadis might be tempted to give evidence against those who corrupted their minds.

I asked the Belgian authorities to give Jay a new identity. His name was synonymous with "jihad" in my country. How could he live, find a job, get married, with that kind of stigma over his head? I felt that he'd done his duty and given a huge amount of evidence to protect the nation from terrorists. So why wouldn't the nation at least give him a chance to live freely? But my pleas fell on deaf ears.

The European press dubbed me the "jihadi hunter." I was proud of the title, mostly because no one else was helping families bring their sons back. Sadly, I was a one-of-a-kind operation. No one else was going to the war zone and doing what I did.

More messages from distraught parents arrived in my Facebook mailbox. Sometimes they were seeking advice about how to deal with a son who was showing jihadi tendencies; sometimes they wanted to know how to get their son back; sometimes they just wanted to share their private pain over a boy who'd turned against everything they'd raised him to be. I tried to give these people hope, and when I came across a case where I thought I might be able to get the son back, I agreed to travel to the Middle East.

I was busy with the case of Lucas's friend, Abdelmalek. The two had been best friends growing up. Abdelmalek's parents were Moroccans—Berbers, actually. A tough people. Idriss and Najat. I went to their house, sat down with them, and went through the same procedure: What are your son's height, weight, Twitter name, distinguishing marks? I had the feeling that this was going to become a routine. Like a murder detective in Chicago and Detroit. A new case every week.

"Did he have any diseases or medical conditions?" I asked.

"He's diabetic," Idriss said.

I noted that. It might be a possible opening. If Abdelmalek couldn't get his medicine in Syria, maybe we could bring him some. An opening gambit.

Idriss, the father, showed me pictures of his boy. Abdelmalek was a handsome guy with an open, smiling face. The morning he disappeared, he was about to leave the house when he told his mother, "Don't expect me for dinner." She thought he was going to one of his friend's houses. The next day, he sent her a picture from Turkey, and said he was heading to Syria. There he took the name Abu Nusaybah al-Baljiki.

Abdelmalek was trying to get other youths to come join him in Raqqa. He posted photos on social media showing him eating pizzas and drinking milkshakes, or the well-stocked shelves of stores in the city, or hanging out with his Belgian friends, guns in hand. It was like the pages of a lifestyle magazine, except it was aimed at potential jihadis. The message was: *Life's great in Raqqa. Wish you were here!*

In contrast to Pol, Abdelmalek's father was a rock. He wasn't afraid of ISIS; in fact, he was royally pissed off at his son, at ISIS, at everything. This was refreshing. He was a fighter and I liked that.

Idriss and I flew to Iraq. The first trip was a complete wash; Abdelmalek wouldn't even agree to meet with his dad. We returned to Belgium, then tried again a month later. We called Abdelmalek on his cell phone as soon as we arrived. Surprisingly, he answered. His father couldn't speak to him anymore; it always ended in arguments. I decided to try. I took the phone and began explaining to Abdelmalek who I was and what I could do for him: I could facilitate him getting out of Syria and back home to Europe in the best possible way for his future.

"Your mother is hurting, Abdelmalek," I said. "You have to consider coming home. This is a disaster for your family."

"If they want to see me, let them come here," he said. "I have nothing more to do with those infidel countries. I would rather die as a martyr than go to a Belgian jail."

"We will fix that with the authorities. Will you consider coming home?"

"Will my parents think about coming here?" he shot back. "That is their duty as Muslims."

His voice dripped with condescension. I'd heard that nonsense one too many times, and I found myself unable to control my temper with him. "You have no respect for your mother!" I shouted. "Your father came all this way to save your ass. He could die here, but you don't give a shit. All you can think about is your buddies and your bullshit."

He shouted back at me. I was an infidel and I should stay out of his business. He did respect his mother, enough to want her to live in a true Islamic state. I wanted to reach through the phone and choke him out.

Apparently, I'd touched a nerve with this guy. I started seeing posts on Facebook and other social media where Abdelmalek was calling for me to be killed. "The head of the traitor's father must roll," and nonsense like that.

It was the first time that a young man I was trying to help had threatened me publicly. I was furious. Here I was in Syria trying to save his sorry ass and he was telling people to murder me. Ironic.

I got Idriss to Raqqa, but it took us ten days to finally get a fix on Abdelmalek's location. Finally, he texted and agreed to meet his father. I made all the arrangements and sent Idriss in alone. I was toxic in ISIS territory; I couldn't accompany him. And with Abdelmalek having such a negative view of my role in all this, it was better I wasn't there anyway.

I sent him with a peace offering: a couple month's supply of his son's diabetes medicine. Almost as soon as he crossed the border, I lost touch with him. There were no more messages from Idriss or Abdelmalek. I kept texting Idriss on WhatsApp and leaving voice mail messages, but it was as if he'd been swallowed up. No communication. I was getting worried. Ten days passed.

Then, a phone call. It was Idriss. He was safe, and he'd been able to meet with Abdelmalek. But the news was anything but good.

Idriss had met his son in a nondescript office building in Raqqa, watched over by armed ISIS guards. The meeting had started off tense; Abdelmalek looked at his father with anger in his eyes. They sat down warily across a table.

"I've brought your medicine," Idriss said, as I'd instructed him. He pushed the package across the table.

Abdelmalek didn't even glance down at the package. He shoved it back to his father.

"I don't need it."

Idriss was knocked off track. "What do you mean? It's for . . ."

"The people here have better medicines."

Idriss looked at his boy helplessly. These crazy loons, running around with guns and RPGs, had somehow developed a finer diabetes medicine than the huge drug companies had, after spending billions of dollars and years of research? Was Abdelmalek out of his mind? If the boy didn't get his insulin, he would die.

Idriss asked him to return home. Abdelmalek didn't reject the offer outright; but he told his father he was worried about getting arrested if he returned to Belgium. It was a good sign; he was actively considering coming back. I'd told Idriss what to say if the topic came up. "Abdelmalek, I spoke to the police," he said, "and they assured me if you return you will not go to prison." That may or may not have been true. (Probably not, as Jay's case showed.) But the truth could wait.

"You're lying," Abdelmalek said.

Idriss pleaded with his son, but it was no use. The connection—the years of trust and love between the two—had been poisoned by ISIS. Idriss left the meeting feeling hopeless.

We returned to Belgium without Abdelmalek, but I told his family not to give up. They had to keep talking to him. They were the young man's only link to reality. No matter how many times he provoked or insulted them, they had to keep that line open.

While we were in Belgium, we got more bad news. A Belgian researcher, Montasser Alde'emeh, traveled to Syria in order to find out why so many youths from our country were fighting for ISIS. He ran across Abdelmalek's name during his work. The young man had put his name on a list of men who wished to become suicide bombers.

The researcher got in touch with Abdelmalek and recorded one of their WhatsApp conversations about the suicide list. We read the transcripts; they are heartbreaking.

Montasser: You should not [volunteer for a suicide mission]. Remove your name from the list.

Abdelmalek: Allah willing, I will carry out a martyrdom operation.

M: Do not blow yourself up, brother. Do not do it. Can't you imagine how sad your parents will be?

A: You are still looking for the truth, unlike me. I found the truth. I kept searching in Belgium and found it.

M: I hate that you are doing that. Don't you realize to what extent I care about you?

A: I don't care. My path to paradise is not in your hands. Whatever you say, I won't listen.

M: Your parents are still Muslims and they want you to return.

A: If they are real believers, they should come here.

What strikes me is the arrogance of this creature that ISIS had created. No one but him and his brothers mattered; everyone else was beneath consideration. I had the feeling that Abdelmalek almost relished causing pain to those who loved him.

Idriss and his wife were disturbed by their son's reaction to their efforts to rescue him. Now that I look back on it, it would have been better, psychologically better, for Idriss never to have seen his son. If he'd remembered him as he once was, it would have been a sweeter memory than the angry, arrogant young man he met in Raqqa. His mother even expressed this thought in an interview with the BBC. "I wish," she said, "everything could go back to the way it once was."

I knew how she felt. Losing your child to ISIS makes even the most trying years of your life look like bliss. And to get so close to restoring that happiness and yet to leave without your son . . . maybe it would have been better that it never happened. I don't know. It haunts me still.

In November 2015, the family got a call. ISIS had announced the martyrdom of their son. It said he'd attacked a convoy of Iraqi military vehicles, blowing himself up and destroying three of them. Everyone inside the vehicles had died. (The Iraqi military denied this, claiming that Abdelmalek had been stopped and been forced to blow himself up away from the convoy.)

Abdelmalek had gotten his wish. He'd become a suicide bomber like his friend Lucas. And his parents were left to imagine his last moments, the terror of them, and then the atomizing of his body, which they'd held in their arms when he was a child.

I see Idriss all the time now. I live in Kortrijk, the same town as him, and we cross paths often. I will see him from afar, recognizing him from the way he walks. He is sadder now. I hug him and whisper in his ear. "Don't forget, you did what you could. Allah decided it had to be this way."

Idriss is trying to forget about Syria. If he focuses on Abdelmalek, he will sink into a pit that he may never get out of, and the family has four other children to take care of. But Najat, his wife, has been destroyed, to put it plainly; she put on a lot of weight after Abdelmalek was killed and has battled a consuming sadness. To this day, she doesn't believe he's really dead. She holds out hope that one day he will come to tap on her window, his eyes filled with remorse.

Chapter Nineteen

THE CALLS POURED IN, FROM all over Europe. *Help us. We are at our wit's end. Nobody is telling us what to do.* I didn't want to go to Syria or Iraq anymore, honestly. I wanted to put that part of my life behind me. Every trip brought back memories of that helpless feeling that had stayed with me for months, of the basement in Kafr Hamra, of the mock execution.

I was divorced now, a single guy. I was a minor celebrity and did some parts in crazy films just to make money. It was a strange life. One day on the set of a film, the next talking to a family whose son had deserted them. On one occasion, I flew from Syria to Belgium after a mission, went to my apartment, stayed eight hours, got a call about another missing boy, and then left again that night. Some days, I thought I was living in a movie, a strange experimental movie about fame and jihad and social media and the craziness of the modern world. But it all came back to the stories of the desperate parents, and despite my exhaustion, I found I couldn't turn them down.

I found Syria more chaotic and fragmented with each trip I made there. The more I saw of the country, the less hope I had for it. Fighting groups would split from their allies and join another group, only to reverse the process and go to war with their new allies. Kurds hated Sunnis who hated Shiites who hated Christians, and so on. I saw no harmony there, and I predict that there will be no peace for at least another generation.

I saw hunger, too. When I had food, either because I'd bought it myself or I'd brought some in with an aid group, I'd give it to poor people on the street. I really loved to do that. Sometimes I dreamt of returning as an aid worker and handing out pallets of food to everyone who needed it. I visited refugee camps and saw the terrible unsanitary conditions there. And I went to the hospitals.

Many times, I walked into a clinic and the wounded mujahideen would look at me in shock. Like "What are *you* doing here?" I was a minor celebrity in Syria, too, and not in a good way. Some of the fighters refused to talk to me: I was a *kafir*, an unbeliever, and I'd spoken out against the brutality of the rebels. The silent ones, I learned, were mostly from ISIS. But I had to go to the hospitals; these fighters were the people who had the freshest information. Often, they'd just left the front lines and they could tell me where the European battalions were at that very moment. I'd give them my phone number so they could text me updates. Where were the toughest checkpoints to get through? Where were the easiest ones? What cities and towns were the European jihadis deployed to? Things I needed to get the Western fighters out.

Many Syrians I met had lost hope themselves. It was ironic. Rebels who told me they hated the West and that the CIA was responsible for the destruction of their country would, in the next breath, ask me if I could get them into Europe. I was like, "What are you talking about—you just said you hated Europe!" But ISIS had changed the war so much that even hardcore fighters were appalled by the indiscriminate violence. ISIS was using barbarian tactics. And these guys wanted out.

I'd estimate that 60 percent of the fighters I met wanted to leave Syria. Long after I'd met them, I'd get texts from deep inside Syria. "Inshallah, Dimitri, how are you? I'm in a bad situation, need to get to Europe. Can you get me a passport or talk to someone in Belgium?" Or: "I'm tired of fighting and want to work and study. Please, Dimitri. How can I get to Germany?" Any pale-faced person they saw, they asked for help. It was heartbreaking. They all dreamt of Europe.

Some of them made it. A few fighters I know are now in Germany or Belgium, having either journeyed there as refugees and gotten permission to stay, or living there illegally. Their lives are difficult: they're waiting for papers, or they're living ten to a tiny room. But it's better than Aleppo or Raqqa. Nobody in Belgium is trying to cut your head off.

Then there were the other messages. A text popped up on my screen one day:

"Hello, I had a contact with the SAVE Association who told me to contact you for me and my family. It has been a year and a half that we search for a way of getting our brother out. The French authorities are aware of the case; we also have a lawyer. But still

we have NO WAY for going out. I have 6 children of young age and 4 wives with me. PLEASE this is URGENT we are in danger. The rebels are coming closer every day and the DAESH [ISIS] forces oblige men to fight and threaten to murder them. And I don't want to see me and my family killed."

These were regular Syrian people caught in the path of ISIS. I could do little for them. I would put the families in touch with refugee agencies, but what they needed was really a military force to go and rescue them, to stop the killing. These texts kept me up at night. People right now, still, are living through things you can't imagine and the fact that they can text you—as if they were a friend asking if you want to go for a beer—makes it seem normal. But it isn't.

When I walked through a street in Aleppo, people would see me and call out, "We need help! Please send us medicines! We want peace in Syria. Help us!" Just outside Aleppo, I was filming a bombing run by an Assad fighter jet on my cell phone. Some jihadis spotted me and they began yelling: "What are you doing? The West isn't helping us, but you're making movies about this? Is it entertainment for you?" There was real venom in their voices. Hatred. But two days later, I was walking through eastern Aleppo and I stopped to talk with some Salafist fighters. They were against the West intervening. That would be imperialism, they told me. They would stay and make a colony out of Syria. These guys didn't want that. "This is our revolution," one of them emphasized.

So you were damned if you did and damned if you didn't. But the majority of the people I met would have received Western help with gratitude. Even the fighters who helped me would talk to me at night. "Why don't they come, Dimitri?" "They" meant the West. I tried to reassure them, but there was little I could say. I knew there was no appetite in places like Belgium for intervention, and it was the same in the U.S.

Another reason for my pessimism was the corruption that I witnessed on every trip. I couldn't count the numbers of oil trucks that were coming out of Syria. Someone was making a lot of money off of each load. One time, I was standing in a Turkish border town when a line of tankers rolled by. I turned to a policeman. "Where is this coming from?" "It's all from Syria," he said with a laugh. "The smugglers buy it cheap from the emirs and then bring it to us." ISIS was making many millions from oil, and the Turks were helping them.

People would ask me when I returned to the West: What is the solution for Syria? As much as it pains me to say, I believe the country should be partitioned. Let Assad and his followers have one part; let the Salafists have another; let the Kurds have their homeland, at last. Otherwise, it's going to be like Israel and Palestine—constant low-level war that sometimes flares up into a real conflagration. The West will be sucked in again and again and no faction would prevail. That could be the motto for the Syria I saw: *No winners.*

Chapter Twenty

THE TRIAL BEGAN IN SEPTEMBER 2014. I went every day to the Palace of Justice in Antwerp, not only to see what had happened to my son, but also to show that his family was with Jay. We needed to show that he was a human being with a past and people who loved him. Who would not give up on him, no matter what.

Before the trial began, Belkacem had released an open letter trying to justify what Sharia4Belgium had done. Through the trial and the letter, I finally got a window into the mind of the man who'd ruined so many lives. In the letter, he was both defiant and crafty. It's a very long document, but I'll quote from the parts that directly affected my son and his fellow believers.

"What I think of Syria and her blessed resistance?" Belkacem asks. "To begin, I ask Allah to stop the bloodshed. May Allah feed the hungry, heal the sick, protect the innocent, and accept the dead as martyrs? The first culprit of the genocide in

Syria, the West, they sponsored and protected the Assad clan for decades.

"So it's not recruiters all over the world who send Muslims to Syria, it's the obvious injustice of the international community. While our media is busy with other issues, the Arab media show daily the suffering of the Syrians. There are three types of Muslims in this case:

1. The 'Muslim' who looks the other way because it is far from him;
2. The Muslim who performs prayers and gives financial support;
3. The Muslim who is going to try to do his bit (through fighting, humanitarian aid, etc.)

Is it terrorism to help your brothers when they have lost all hope in humanity? The extremists were not terrorists when they fought against the Russians in Afghanistan or against the Serbs in Bosnia. The old argument is the political agenda of some rebels. They want to establish an Islamic state in Syria. I say, 'So what!'"

He was right, I think, about this. If the people of the Middle East wanted to create a religious caliphate, that was their business, so long as they respected the human rights of the people who lived in it. But Belkacem glossed over the obvious truth: the citizens of Iraq and Syria never voted to live in such a place, never asked for ISIS to rule their lives in such a medieval way. ISIS was imposed on them through violence.

Then he goes on:

"The Belgian politicians, media, and judiciary have created the illusion that recruiters are brainwashing young people to send them ultimately to conflict. It makes sense on the one hand that such idiotic nonsense is spreading. How else can they spread the Islamophobic, racist, and discriminatory attitude of the Belgian state?

"I support the revolutions in the Islamic world, from Rabat to Jakarta. . . . Unfortunately, the reality is that I have neither the authority nor the status to send people to the east or west. . . .

"A lot of practicing Muslims feel every day the injustice of the government and society. . . . Many went to Syria to lead a new life. This is the case of many converts and young Muslims. The fact that young people prefer to live under bombs than in the 'warm welcoming Flanders' in itself is another proof against the government. Everything is apparently better than Belgium. . . .

"Sharia4Belgium was popular among the Muslims, so we were terrorists. Massive searches and arrests. Lies, distortions, and misinterpretations were used to put a lawsuit together. The media was used to spread propaganda against us."

By the time I finished reading the letter, I was furious. He outright lied about his intentions toward people like my son. There was brainwashing going on; and they did encourage young men to go fight in Syria. It infuriated me that he was trying to evade responsibility for his work, which left so many broken families and wasted lives behind.

For Belkacem and his brothers, the West was to blame for everything. We were the warmongers, we were the terrorists, we were the ones who used violence to achieve our aims. He took no responsibility for what he'd done. His own vanity shines out through the pages of his letter, but remorse is nowhere to be found.

As the trial progressed, I kept encountering the fallout from Belkacem and people like him. The calls came in from all over Europe: *My son is missing, have you seen him? My son wants to come home but is afraid of a long jail sentence; what should he do? My son is dead. Bring me anything you can find of him.*

A call came in from a mother in Denmark. ISIS had told her that her child had been killed in Kobane, blown apart by an American bomb. The mother wanted something from him—his phone, a boot, clothes, even a bone fragment—to bury. I don't know if she wanted it as proof that her son was gone or as a memento to remember him by. Perhaps both.

I got hold of my contacts in Syria. "If he'd been killed by a bullet, it might be possible," one of them said. "But a bomb? There's probably nothing of him left, and if there is, it's mixed in with the fighters who died with him." I had to call the mother and tell her that there was no chance. Her voice on the phone was filled with sadness.

Another case, also from Denmark, this time Copenhagen. For this one, I actually went to the Syrian border. The boy had been messaging his mother, saying he was unhappy with ISIS. They'd moved him from an area near Kobane to another battlefield, and he was upset about that. Perhaps his friends were near the Kobane sector; perhaps the new area was too dangerous. I don't know. But he was refusing to fight and his mother sensed an opening. She asked me to go. I flew to Turkey and went to the border.

I was calling the son, telling him that I was on the way to see him. But he was resisting. "You're an infidel," he told me. He even sent me a selfie of him wearing a suicide belt. He was torn. He didn't want to be in Syria, but he was afraid to return home, sure that he would be thrown in prison.

I can't tell you how many young Western fighters told me the same thing: if they could return home and be free, they would leave the war. It was this stupid policy that was keeping them in Syria. "Your mother is waiting for you," I told this fighter. "We'll make sure you don't go to prison." But he wouldn't listen.

Our final conversation came a few weeks later. He called me to say that ISIS was sending him into the no man's area between their front lines and the Kurdish *peshmerga* troops. They were tired of his refusals to do battle. Either he went or they would kill him themselves. I called Copenhagen and relayed the news. His parents were frantic.

"Can you go get him? What should we do?" There was nothing to do. We had to wait and see if by some miracle he survived the no man's land.

The day after our conversation, someone rang the parents' bell. It was the Islamist radical who'd recruited their son to ISIS. He told the couple he was sorry to disturb them, but he wanted to tell them that he'd just gotten bad news. "Your son is dead."

I can imagine they wanted to take that man by his throat

and finish him off right there. He wasn't ashamed of what he'd done. He was simply performing a bureaucratic function. The father cried day and night. He called his son's cell phone, but ISIS had given it to another fighter. This young man hung up on the father after he spoke a few words.

The family wanted the son's body returned to them. I spoke to my Syrian contacts and asked them to try. The Kurds controlled the area. Their fighters had crawled over every inch of that territory. I was able to find out the exact building where the son had been killed. When they called me back, they told me that the Kurdish fighters said they were not in the business of returning ISIS fighters to their families. When they came across dead jihadis, they either burned the bodies or opened a ditch with a tractor and piled them in.

The boy's father decided to go to Kobane. We took him to the tallest building in the city so he could see the place where his son had died. That was the closest he could get to his son's body. He stared out at the ruined buildings and cried.

Chapter Twenty-One

I WAS IN SYRIA WORKING on the case of a missing Dutch kid when my driver, Farouk, called me. Farouk was an immense help to me in Syria; many of his family members belonged to Jabhat al-Nusra and his information was like gold.

"There is a Belgian here, very bad shape. He wants to go home. Are you interested?"

"Of course!" I said. "Where is he?"

The young man was in a clinic near Reyhanli, Turkey. I went to see him. The hospital was a bare-bones affair, with dirty linen on the beds and not enough nurses. I found Malek lying on a cot, his leg propped up. He was emaciated, almost a skeleton. The ribs were sticking through the skin, and I could see the lines of his jawbone clearly. The young man was twenty-four; his parents had emigrated to Belgium from Africa and he had become radicalized in a mosque there.

Malek had been wounded when a bomb dropped near him. The shrapnel had ripped through his leg. His brothers had brought him to this hospital for treatment; actually, it would be more accurate to say they'd abandoned him in the hospital. Not once had they come back to check on him or to see that he was getting the proper care.

The guy was pissed off. His leg was in terrible shape. I didn't like the look of it. "Look how I am here suffering and almost dead," he said to me. "I came here to help the Syrians win their freedom, and this is how they treat me. Where are all my brothers and sisters?"

It was a sad story. He'd been in the hospital for months.

I got his father's number and called him. Roger hadn't seen or had word of his son for a year. He was overjoyed when I told him I was sitting in a hospital in Turkey and Malek was five feet away from me. "It's a gift from God," he told me.

But Malek was badly injured and his wounds were festering. We had to get him out. I called the Belgian embassy and they agreed to issue Malek papers to return home. For once, the possibility of prison was irrelevant. Malek didn't even ask about it; he was willing to do anything to get out of this sweltering hellhole.

Roger flew to Istanbul and then made it to the clinic. The Belgian government had agreed to take his son back, but that didn't mean he was free to leave. ISIS still had claims on him, even if they'd left him to rot in the hospital. And Roger didn't want to wait for the Belgian government to arrange for transportation. His son could be dead by then. So how to get him out?

Roger and I decided to try to smuggle Malek out. The hospital had only a few doctors and one or two guards. One afternoon, Roger went to Malek's room with a wheelchair. He lifted his bone-thin son out of the bed, nearly crying at how light he was, and maneuvered him into the chair. He then wheeled him down the hallway and out the front door into the sunshine.

We had a car waiting. They opened the trunk and bundled Malek in. Then they shut it and headed for the border.

Simple and quick. Roger drove him to the Bulgarian border. There, the guards took one look at the nervous Roger and decided to inspect the car. They opened the trunk and found Malek.

Big problem. The young man had no papers. We finally got him to Belgium, where he was treated for his wounds. He had to do a year in jail. After he got out of prison, Malek married a Belgian girl. I was so happy for him.

I see his father often now in Belgium. I love running into him. His son was my first real success story after Jay.

I ran across all kinds of characters in Syria and Iraq. One of the more memorable was Abu Saif. His case showed how Western governments let valuable intelligence assets slip through their hands out of sheer fear. It was also a tragedy that didn't have to happen.

Abu Saif had been a chef in Belgium when the extremist bug bit him. He was working in a restaurant; one day he happened to be browsing through YouTube and came on a video which was alleged to show Syrian soldiers massacring a group of children. Abu Saif was devastated. He vowed to leave Belgium and go fight these monsters.

Abu Saif and his younger brother journeyed to Turkey, then snuck into Syria like so many other fighters had before him. They went looking for the most powerful group at the time, and they found Jabhat al-Nusra. Abu Saif and his brother joined a seventy-member battalion and saw intense action on the streets of Aleppo and Idlib. "I saw fighters from all around the world," he said. He was inspired by the movement, and called his friends back home, telling them they must come to the battlefield to fight for Syrians. "I did it and I'm proud of it." He was like a radical Pied Piper playing his flute from Syria. Eventually, his wife and his mother made the trip. But by then he'd grown disillusioned.

Abu Saif contacted me to say that he was leaving al-Nusra and wanted to go back to Belgium. Could I help?

I thought it was a trap. What if this was ISIS finally reaching out to finally kill me? I didn't think I was high on their list of targets, not at all, but I thought I'd made that list, or a sublist of at least one of its battalions. I was reluctant to meet Abu Saif, but eventually he convinced me that he was sincere. He crossed the border, fleeing al-Nusra, and came to my hotel.

He was a big fat guy with a lot of energy—a little manic, to be honest. After all Syrian fighters had done for me, I felt obliged to help this guy who wanted to change his life. Sitting on my hotel bed, he told me the constant fighting and hardship had taken their toll on his family. First his wife left, but she found herself unable to get back into Belgium; officials there worried she'd been radicalized. Instead, she landed in Morocco. Next, his younger brother went and was arrested before being put into a Dutch prison.

Abu Saif told me he was done with al-Nusra and wanted nothing more than to see his mother again. I asked him why he went to Syria. He told me that he'd been struggling with life in Belgium; money was tight, and he couldn't find a job. He'd experienced racism. He applied for so many restaurants jobs; he had the skills and the knowledge to be a good employee but he never seemed to be chosen for the good positions. When he saw the videos from Syria, he actually thought he would have a better life there. It wasn't really about ideology, the way he explained it; it was about being treated fairly and having some opportunities.

"So what happened in Syria? "I asked. He made a face. He couldn't get along with anyone in al-Nusra; there was political infighting almost from the day he got there. He and his friends were being ordered to fight people with whom he had no argument, and things got chaotic. The chain of command broke down, and bands of jihadis began going off on their own.

I felt Abu Saif was sincere and could be an excellent informant for one of the Western intelligence agencies. I called around. My contact at the American embassy said, "No deal; he's not one of ours." But they tried their best to help. They even brought him in for an interview. The Belgian embassy in Turkey stonewalled me; they thought he might blow up something in Brussels. "But this guy knows *everyone*," I told them. "He'd be an amazing asset—his phone alone must contain clues that it would take you a year to get in any other way."

After weeks of trying, I had to call Abu Saif and tell him the bad news. No one wanted him. "What if I snuck back into Belgium?" he asked.

"Let's find out," I said.

We called the Belgian police and got a mid-level official on the line. "What happens if I come back?" Abu-Saif asked.

The guy hemmed and hawed but eventually gave Abu Saif a number: five years. That was the minimum he would spend in prison.

It was crazy. Abu Saif had rebelled against extremism and he could have gone to schools and online telling other young Muslims not to go to Syria. But the Belgians were too scared to take even the small risk he represented. Abu Saif had nowhere left to go. He told me he was thinking of joining ISIS. "There are plenty of Belgians in the organization," he told me. "I recruited half of them!" He was laughing when he said this. I told him going to the Islamic State would be a mistake. He'd killed ISIS members in Aleppo. If he tried to join them, the group would think he was a spy and they'd execute him. I'd seen it happen before.

"Dimitri, my friend," he said, "they will roll out the red carpet for me. You watch."

I tried one last gambit. I arranged an exclusive with Abu Saif for a Belgian news channel. Maybe the publicity would help. But in it, Abu Saif seemed to have given up hope of ever making it back to Europe. "So many of my friends joined ISIS," he later told a reporter. "I will do the same. We are brothers in Islam. We will share everything together. We will eat together, pray together, sleep together, and of course fight together."

He wanted to go home, but instead he went to ISIS. Weeks later, Abu Saif was captured by the police at the Turkish-Syrian border. Turkey ended up exchanging him for thirty-five ISIS prisoners, and he was released into the Islamic State's hands. I saw pictures of him on Facebook with a bomb belt strung across his waist. He was smiling. So he'd made it after all.

Chapter Twenty-Two

IN LATE NOVEMBER, 2014, I gave an interview to a British newspaper. I felt I could no longer keep quiet about what I was hearing and seeing in Syria. I had to do something about it.

Fighters there were telling me that ISIS was going to attack Europe. At first, when my contacts told me such things, I couldn't believe it. I thought they were bullshitting me to feel important, or to make their fighting groups look more powerful than they were. But the longer I spoke with them, the more I saw how deep their conviction that the West was attacking Muslims, and needed to be hurt in return, really was.

I was dumbfounded. Yes, there were French airplanes in the sky, but the whole origin of the Civil War was Syrian. It had been born here and nurtured by the hatred and oppression fueled by the Assad regime. The West hadn't created Assad or the Islamist fighters who opposed him. And yet the men I met said things like, "The CIA is involved," or "Europe is supporting tyrants and we must strike back." Utter madness.

These fighters weren't lying to me, of that I was convinced. They were warning me. They even told me that ISIS was sending people secretly, as refugees, into the countries of the European Union.

When I talked to people at home about this, I found complacency. No one wanted to face the threat. There had been small incidents in places like Toulouse and Brussels, but these were nothing compared to what Islamic terrorists were capable of doing, what they wanted to do. And so I had to speak out.

"It's not the kids who are the principal danger," I told a newspaper. "It's the chiefs whom you never see in the videos. The mature men running this organization are deeply sinister and extremely well-funded, and they have European countries such as Britain, France, and Belgium in their sights."

I'd heard it from both Salafists and secular fighters in Syria. The jihadis and their leadership were angry at Western meddling in their caliphate, and they weren't going to take it lying down. "Their aim is to take revenge against the West for what they view as an all-out assault on them, and they will strike when they are ready. I've been told by very influential sources that they have sleeper cells over here, and are preparing to unleash their war on Europe."

What could be done, the newspaper asked? I said there needed to be an international mission to shut down Salafist websites, as they were the point of the spear for radicalization. There had to be stricter controls on young people trying to travel to and from Turkey. I also told the reporter that I was getting no support for my efforts to bring young fighters back from Syria, and that it was time for an organization that could provide funds and policies for rescuing those who sincerely wanted to come back. "The priority has to be to save our children."

For the wider problem, I told journalists that we had to face facts: In order to crack down on extremists, we were going to have to curb our rights. We had to beef up the resources of our intelligence agencies, give them wider access to communications and stronger powers to investigate people. We had to tighten border controls, especially when it came to teenagers or youths traveling alone. I knew that several times when jihadis heading to Syria had been stopped in Istanbul and questioned—"What are you doing here alone?"—they'd answered as they'd been taught to: "We're meeting our families for a wedding." And they were let through. That had to stop.

There was, at the time, a ridiculous law in Belgium that forbade any police raids on houses between 10:00 P.M. and 5:00 A.M. Can you even fathom the absurdity of such a thing? The law had been instituted in 1969 and couldn't be gotten around except in cases of "flagrant crimes of fire." It was a law for another era, a more innocent time.

Critics said I was an Islamophobe and an alarmist. They accused me of being a right-winger. I am nothing of the sort. I believe in the equality of all peoples and that all citizens must be treated with respect. I'm trying to protect those rights, not get rid of them. The ones who want those beautiful privileges to disappear are the Islamists. If they are preaching violence and the overthrowing of the state, they should be deported if they are immigrants and imprisoned if they are Belgians.

A month and a half after the interview, radicals struck Paris, killing twenty people. Ten months after that, it was Paris again, with 137 dead, 7 of them terrorists. Two days after the second massacre, Belgian police learned that one of the suspected extremists, Salah Abdeslam, was staying in a house in the largely Muslim neighborhood of Molenbeek. They got this information late in the evening.

What did they do? Did they go and get Abdeslam and ask him if any more attacks were planned? Did they arrest him?

No. A raid would have been in violation of the 1969 law. They stayed out of Molenbeek until the next morning. When they went to the apartment, Abdeslam was gone.

Things are getting better, slowly. When I travel now, I see more soldiers in the airports and in public places. There needs to be more. ISIS is being degraded but its ideology is still strong.

We need ex-fighters to tell young people that ISIS is selling a fake vision, that the world of justice and heroism you see in their videos doesn't really exist. But only someone who's been to Syria and Iraq can convince a sixteen-year-old who believes the propaganda. Returning jihadis, if they're properly vetted and de-radicalized, can become some of our best weapons against extremism.

What I want to tell people in the West is that radical Islam is not going to give up. America has already seen a number of its young men and women radicalized. Some of them have ended up with ISIS—people you may not have heard of. Douglas McAuthur McCain converted to Islam in 2004 and soon started calling himself "Abu Jihad the American." He went to Syria and took up arms with the extremists. Five months after he'd arrived, he was killed in a gunfight with the Free Syrian Army. Online, he'd written what could have served as his epitaph: "It's Islam over everything."

Think about that. *Islam over everything.* That speaks to a deep, lasting belief. And there have been other young Americans who shared it. One blew himself up in a suicide attack in Syria in 2014. Others have risen to become important spokesmen for the group.

I've been on the front lines. I've looked into the eyes of these young men. And I've held the hands of parents who said, "I didn't think it could happen to my family."

It can. ISIS is in your hometown—if not in the person of a recruiter, then in the incredibly powerful presence of radical websites. They are looking for vulnerable and idealistic young people to capture for their cause. No one is immune.

The West is no longer asleep. But it still doesn't want to face the truth about ISIS and other Islamic radicals. They're thinking years ahead. They're very well funded. They will carry on the battle for generations. And what happened to my family will happen to many more American families, unless you take measures to defeat it.

What can we do?

I'd love to see bigger budgets for our intelligence and security agencies. What kind of infrastructure do these outfits have in places where extremism breeds, like Syria and Iraq? From what I saw, very little. Intelligence officials need informants, guys on the ground, as well as things like cutting-edge tracking gear. This will cost money. We need to spend it wisely, but we need to spend it.

When I was in Syria, I saw how oil finances terror. Every tanker-load of the black stuff that flows across the Turkish–Syria border means more suicide vests, more RPGs and AK-47s for the extremists. We need to make it clear to the Turks and to any company that does business with these shady operators paying ISIS for oil that we are dead serious about stopping them. If you play with the extremists, you'll get you banned from legitimate markets. Raise the price on cooperation with terror. And raise it high.

But we can't just be constantly reacting to threats. We have to lean forward. In schools where students have been radicalized, we should have programs on what to look for and how to counter the mind games that recruiters play. The good news is that there is a blueprint that these men follow time and time again; you can predict the kids they'll go after and you can predict their methods. This gives us a tactical advantage over the recruiters, but we aren't using it. We're waiting for the disaster before asking ourselves how it happened.

People say to me: All of this sounds a little scary. Do we want to live in a police state? Do we have to feel we are being watched every time we step out in public?

Effective surveillance doesn't have to add up to a police state. You can crack down on terrorists without obliterating personal liberties, but you do have to curtail them at certain times, in certain areas. And after what I've gone through, my sincere opinion is that it's worth the sacrifice. My question to the doubters is: Do you want to lose a generation to radicals? Is that worth your privacy?

Chapter Twenty-Three

IN FEBRUARY 2015 IT WAS announced that a judgment had been reached in the Sharia4Belgium trial. I was nervous. Jay was nervous. Helen even more so.

We headed to the Palace of Justice, a beautiful steel-and-glass structure that seemed to broadcast the openness of European society, to hear the verdict. The month before, gunmen in Paris had slaughtered innocents in the latest Islamist outrage. You could feel the tension in the court: Was Europe going to stand up to these bastards or not?

They were. The judge declared that Sharia4Belgium was a terrorist organization and had helped recruit dozens of Belgians for fighting groups in Syria. All but one of the forty six members—including Fouad Belkacem—were convicted. "Belkacem is responsible for the radicalization of young men to prepare them for Salafist combat, which has as its core no place for democratic values," the judge said in his decision. Belkacem, wearing a green jumpsuit, with handcuffs and a thick restraint around his waist, got twelve years; some of the others got between three and fifteen. When asked if he had anything to say, Belkacem whispered, "I am a Muslim, not a terrorist."

"Liar!" someone cried out. I turned to find the speaker. It was Ozana, the mother of the boy who'd been recruited by Belkacem and died in Syria. I looked over and saw the pain in her face. I knew why she'd cried out; I knew her struggle.

But at last Belkacem would be going to prison for many years. And my son had helped put him there. I felt a sense of fulfillment.

Jay received forty months, but his sentence was suspended and he was able to walk free out of that courtroom. We left the Palace of Justice walking on air, our heads held high. This part of our life, I thought, is over.

I was too optimistic. Around the time of the trial, a journalist from *The New Yorker* came to write a story about Jay and Sharia4Belgium. He interviewed my son and found out some shocking things. Jay told him that he still believed in the idea of the caliphate, which was in his view "something which you can't stop or hold back." He said that he was still radicalized. From the article, I learned that Jay took pains to trick me in small ways. When he was with me, he wore Western clothes, jeans and sweaters. When he was not, he donned a *qamis,* a long Islamic shirt that often reaches to the ankles.

Even more stunning things followed. Jay even refused to condemn the killing of James Foley, though he didn't praise it.

For Jay, it was something to be decided by Islamic scholars. He said that he still believed most of what Belkacem had taught him and that he could even go back to Syria without being punished by ISIS. "People think I can't go there, because I'll get killed," he said. But he argued that his testifying against Sharia4Belgium would have no effect on his reception by Syrian extremists.

I was shocked and heartbroken. Had we gone through all this only to have Jay remain an unrepentant radical? And to be so naive to think that ISIS would welcome him back with open arms? It was so disturbing that it made me sick to think about it.

My only hope was that the guilt of turning against his comrades had caused Jay to turn defiant. Perhaps he felt trapped into testifying and this was his way of atoning, though there was nothing to atone for.

My son had been given very little time to wash the sickness out of his heart. He'd gone from fighting in Syria to a police interrogation room with only a small break. There was no time to sort out fact from fiction.

I knew that the battle wasn't over; I had saved Jay's body, but now I had to help heal his mind. Meanwhile, there were more families that wanted my expertise; my phone was constantly buzzing with new requests. I needed to resume my jihadi-hunting.

How does one end up in the Islamic State? There are a hundred roads: love, debt, a search for identity, bad luck.

Laura Passoni fell victim to the first. A Belgian citizen from a Catholic family, she'd converted to Islam as a teenager, largely because her best friend was a believer. "I was not forced to become a Muslim," she said. "I was persuaded." At twenty-nine, she was a single mother working in a supermarket in the city of Charleroi. The father of her child had left her. "My husband met another woman and left me and abandoned his little boy," she said. "I went into a deep depression."

While chatting online, she met Osama, a Tunisian guy. "He told me I could be a nurse and help the Syrian people. He told me I could start my life all over again." Osama sensed what Laura needed and wanted to hear. "He made me believe in my dreams." The two met and fell in love. The family accepted the young man and Laura and Osama were married within weeks of meeting.

The whole family went for a cruise in the Mediterranean, what should have been a relaxing trip filled with memories of sunsets and family meals. They stopped in Venice and then sailed on to Turkey. There, Osama took his wife off the boat and told her they were moving to Syria.

Laura didn't protest. She was deeply in love with this man; she compared the experience to standing underneath a waterfall, whose constant pressure eventually wore you down, or "washed you away." From a cosmopolitan Belgian, she'd transformed herself into a "jihadi bride."

The couple moved to the city of al-Bab, near Aleppo, in 2014, with Laura's son from a previous marriage. Laura had completely bought in to the myth of the Islamic State: that it was the one place in the world that one could live a true Muslim life. In addition, there were no taxes, free health care, and a range of "Islamic" medicines you could never get in a Belgian pharmacy.

Women did have some rights in the Islamic State, but they were few and far between. If a single woman comes to the caliphate, she has to stay in a secret location, a house occupied by other single women. They can't be forced to marry anyone; the choice is theirs alone. But without a husband, they are prisoners of the state, so many marry the first man who comes along, simply to escape this fate. It's the same when a husband is killed or dies; there's a period of mourning and, once that's finished, no one can force them to marry again. They are presented with other jihadis who are looking for wives. Their status has increased, but they aren't free.

Once Laura and her family were settled in al-Bab, she began to sense the truth. She couldn't leave the house and was forced to spend her whole days cooking and cleaning. She could only walk outside when accompanied by her husband, and only if she was dressed in a burka. She'd been used to going wherever she wanted in Europe, to making her own decisions. Just walking to the grocery store was now a major undertaking, and she felt the freedom she'd taken for granted shrivel.

Laura met other European women who'd been persuaded to come to Syria from France and Germany. "Why women? Because we make babies and especially boys, the future cubs of the caliphate, as they say. They need descendants." The women had moved to Syria for many of the reasons she had: to follow a lover, to find meaning, to change their boring lives. But others had less pleasant reasons for being there. "There were plenty of women who were full of hatred. All they wanted to do was get a Kalashnikov and launch attacks."

The caliphate wasn't the place Laura had imagined. She walked through the city square and saw newly crucified bodies hanging on their wooden crosses. She was horrified to see that some mothers actually let their children go up to the corpses and touch them. For the first time, she began to think about what effect such sights and experiences were having on her son.

Passoni found that the job she'd been promised, that of a nurse, was not going to happen. Instead, she was told to cook and clean for a Syrian family. During this time, she became pregnant with her second child and soon became a prisoner in her own home. "I was forbidden to do anything," she remembered. Even surfing the Net or sending an e-mail to her family, which missed her terribly, was forbidden, unless her husband was sitting next to her. As the months went by, Laura thought constantly about her young son, who would soon go to an ISIS-controlled school. Would the Islamic State groom him into an extremist, or even a suicide bomber?

"I didn't want him to be like them. I didn't want him to be a terrorist. It was at that moment that I decided 'I can't do it.'" So she hatched a plan to get out.

First she acquired a cell phone. She texted her parents, Pascal and Antoinette, and told them that she was having second thoughts and wanted to leave. She also began to work on Osama, who'd become a bookkeeper for ISIS. Her husband was still committed to the caliphate, though he admitted that he was having doubts.

Laura's parents called me. Could I help get her out? *Of course,* I said, *we will try.* But freeing a woman from ISIS control is even harder than saving a jihadi. At least a man has some freedom to travel. A single woman, alone? Almost impossible. Even if you're traveling in a car, you need a man next to you to confirm that he's given his permission.

I told them to ask her emir for a pass. Only someone recognized by the Islamic State could issue permission to get out of the caliphate. The emir refused. The state wanted to keep all the childbearing women they could, and so she wasn't allowed to leave.

I traveled to Turkey with Laura's father, Pascal. He was an older man with a short gray beard. Somewhat frail. I had doubts about bringing him to the border. What if he witnessed Laura being pulled out of a car and whipped? I wondered if, physically, he could take that, or even the day-to-day stress of searching for his daughter.

"You're very brave to be doing this," I said. He just looked at me and smiled, as if to say, *And what else can I do?*

I knew al-Bab; it could only be reached by passing through two heavily guarded ISIS checkpoints. Osama approached the emir and asked for a pass for his wife; he still wanted to stay. The man refused.

Laura said she wanted to try to leave even without permission from her emir. On the phone, she became distraught. "I have to get out now!" she shouted at me. We decided to try with her and her child.

I sent Yusuf, my best contact in Syria, to see her. He noted everything she was wearing and texted it to us at the border, so that we would recognize her once she arrived there. Then he called her a taxi; he couldn't accompany her, because he wasn't her husband or her close relative. Laura got into the car with her son. She was incredibly nervous. She knew the price for attempting to flee the Islamic State without permission: whippings, at the very least.

At the first checkpoint, the guard only glanced at the taxi before waving it through. Now all that remained was the last, outer barrier. When the driver pulled up, the guard, armed with a Kalashnikov, bent down and studied Laura. He asked her what she was doing traveling without her husband. She made some excuse, but her nerves were showing and the man pulled her out of the taxi, berating her for breaking the laws of the Islamic State. He began slapping and beating her in front of her own child. Another guard grabbed the young boy and smacked him in the face. All the while, they were shouting questions.

The child, who was now five, began to babble, "Papi, Papi," the name he spoke to his grandfather on the phone. The guards heard this and began to interrogate the child: Who was Papi? The boy told him he was going to see his grandfather. The game was up. Laura managed to hide the phone from the fighters, the day's only victory.

I was forty minutes away, waiting in Kilis at the Turkish border. I feared for Laura's life at that moment. ISIS was mercurial;

they could let her go or they could whip her in the public square or even execute her.

As it turned out, Laura was lucky. The guards contacted Osama and told him to come retrieve his wife. They brought her back to her apartment and put a guard outside her door. She was now truly a captive.

Time passed. We could try nothing until ISIS stopped watching her so closely. But Laura was texting her parents, saying that the bombing from Assad's forces was getting closer. She was still pregnant with her second child and was afraid an explosive would hit her house one day and kill the whole family.

Again, Osama went to the emir he knew and asked for a pass. "By Allah," the man said, "if you ask me again, I will kill you." Perhaps the emir didn't want to let him go because he was a bookkeeper and knew the caliphate's financial secrets. But the answer was no and it wasn't possible to ask again.

I got on the phone with Osama. "Tell the authorities that your wife is having pains with the pregnancy. The baby is endangered. You want to get her to a clinic in Turkey." He told me he'd tried that, but the answer came back: the Islamic State had the best medical facilities in the world, there was no need to go anywhere. These fantasists actually believed their own nonsense. He handed the phone to Laura. "Please get me across the border!" she shouted. I tried to tell her we were working on it, but it was difficult. It was months before we heard from her again.

In April 2015, our second chance came. By then, Osama had been convinced that it was time to leave. I gave Laura the exact route she had to follow to get out. Karkamis was the only town where they didn't have guards standing at the border. "You need to do this in the daytime," I said. At night, the guards wouldn't let her pass. The deadline to make it through was 6:00 P.M.

I knew that ISIS was still checking on Laura. If they happened to knock on her door on the day she escaped, they would immediately go looking for her.

Pascal and I waited at Karkamis, our nerves keyed up. Cars would pull up and then drive off. Yusuf was waiting in the crowd of onlookers on the Syrian side, watching each vehicle.

A taxi pulled up. A woman got out, but it wasn't Laura.

Another. This time we realized it was Laura's car. But there was something wrong; the guards weren't letting her pass.

My phone rang.

"Where is Yusuf?" Laura cried. She was almost frantic. "I don't see him. They're not letting us through!"

I couldn't say anything. Yusuf had spotted Laura, but he didn't want to draw attention by approaching her. If there were ISIS operatives at the crossing, they could still grab her and send her back to be tortured.

I told her just to keep coming forward. To walk.

Pascal, Laura's father, was with me. He was talking a blue streak, constantly asking what was going on, a nervous wreck. Finally, we saw Laura, holding her infant in her arms, ahead of us with the rest of her family. She was in Turkish territory and wearing a huge smile.

We ran to her. Pascal grabbed her in an embrace, sobbing. He'd been a desperate refugee after World War II before finding asylum in Belgium; he knew what it meant to live in terror. I, too, was crying. To have gotten a family out of the hell of the caliphate . . . I felt like I'd helped redeem three human beings. Now they could live their lives as they saw fit.

Laura and Osama flew back to Brussels and were arrested at the airport. She was convicted of joining a terrorist organization and received a suspended sentence with strict probation. She can't touch a computer or have a passport. She can't contact her ex-husband for a number of years; her children were taken away from her temporarily and given to her parents. But, for Laura, it was worth it. "I accepted the punishment," she said. "To be honest, it was a relief compared to the hell I went through in Syria."

Now Laura goes to schools to warn children about falling for the Islamist's lies. She says she has become a different person and wants to live a normal life in freedom. "Because I saw death very close, as did my child . . . my six-year-old, I have explained to him . . . the mistake I made, and ask for his forgiveness. And when he's bigger, I will teach him to live the truth and not fall into a trap like this."

Osama got four years. She is not bitter toward him; after all, he was crucial to her escape. As for her young son, the real reason for her escape, she's found that he's forgotten much of what he saw in Syria.

Laura, like me, got lucky.

Chapter Twenty-Four

AT HOME, JAY WAS STRUGGLING. My plan for integrating him back into his life wasn't working out the way I'd hoped.

Going out in public was a trial. He'd be walking down the street and men and women would stop in their tracks and stare at him as if trying to place him. He dreaded these moments, these split seconds between the moment they recognized him as someone famous and the moment when they realized that no, he wasn't a soccer star or a rapper or an actor but was in fact that boy who joined ISIS. "Hey, you're the one who went to Syria!" they'd call out. Some meant no harm—Jay had achieved a kind of notoriety and this was the product of it. But many of them did.

It happened every day. Literally, every day. He'd be walking through the shopping district of Antwerp and he'd hear someone shout "Terrorist!" He would whirl around and the faces surrounding him would have these little smiles of recognition. *Who said it?* He couldn't tell. It was amazing how many people knew my son's face. And amazing how much they hated him.

I begged the government to help. In Denmark, returning fighters were taken into a de-radicalization program and given a place to live and a small income or a job as they tried to get back on their feet. This allowed them to resume a normal life without falling back into the thinking that had gotten them radicalized in the first place. But in Belgium, there was nothing. *Zilch*.

Jay went to look for a job. He would have taken anything; he wanted to work, for the self-respect and discipline it would bring as much as the money. But when he walked into a store and began filling out the application, the manager would come over and say, "Aren't you that guy I read about in the news?" Jay would have to admit, "Yes, it's me." The first time it happened, the manager said nothing more and told Jay they would call him if a spot came open. Jay waited but no call ever came.

He didn't give up. Whenever he saw a sign in a window, he would go in. Restaurants, retail shops, delivery services. Whatever, just give me a job and let me prove how hard I can work. But no one would give him a shot. If you're a former thief or embezzler or a guy who likes to get into brawls on Saturday night, fine, you can start again. But not former jihadis.

I was distraught. I watched the sons and daughters of my friends beginning their careers, learning new skills and making a little money for a down payment on a house. But Jay was standing still. The government hadn't put him in prison after the trial, but he spent every day in a wider jail, one with no release date.

Jay began to think his appearance was the problem: He still had the beard and the locked hair that he'd had in Syria. So he shaved both of them off, and started to wear eyeglasses. *I'm willing to start fresh,* he was saying. *I turned in Belkacem and testified against Sharia4Belgium. I've agreed that I made a mistake. I've changed my looks. What else can I do?*

But nothing worked. Somehow, people still recognized him. Jay applied for more than a hundred jobs in the years after he returned, but never got a single offer.

There were going to be no second chances for my son.

In my paranoid moments, I imagined that my country *wanted* Jay to fail. They wanted to drive him back into the arms of the Islamic radicals, so they could say: *See? These people never change. They cannot be trusted, and we did the right thing by rejecting him.*

Jay was the key to convicting the Sharia4Belgium radicals, and yet the society he protected still called him a terrorist. Even today, in this book, I can't publish a photo of what he currently looks like, because the security services have told me that it will endanger his life. The extremists would post it online and mention that it would be good if he was dead, and one of their followers would go looking for him with a knife or a gun. Even now, when I go online, I see this beautiful picture of Jay and myself embracing after his rescue, and underneath it: "He chose the camp of the enemy." Or: "Jejoen, you will never have a second's rest in your entire life." Or: "Your head must be cut off."

I regularly find radical websites that offer instructions on how to spot Jay. "Sometimes wears nerd glasses," wrote one, "and has shaved his head." These are tips for assassins. I even get texts from fighters in Syria reminding me that they are still looking for him. One of them showed a picture of a jihadi's shoe with my son's passport resting on it. "Come to take your baby's passport," the message read. I knew the jihadi who sent it. He and his brothers haven't forgotten my son.

Jay was caught in a no-man's-land. He'd renounced his past but he couldn't move forward. And I was forced to watch it happen.

Not long after I'd returned from the Laura Passoni mission, I was contacted by an official high up in the Peruvian government. The son of a prominent family there had run off to Iraq to join ISIS. *My God*, I thought, *Peru?* There's no way the jihadi poison has spread that far. But it was true.

I spoke with the family. They told me about the boy. He'd been a student at a good school when an American convert to Islam had begun to groom him for jihad. Baseball was the young man's favorite sport, and apparently the American had used that love to connect with him.

The boy had a psychological issue; he was schizophrenic. Part of his illness was the tendency to "see monsters all around him." The illness was under control; the young man had been receiving therapy and medication. But the recruiter had used the sickness against him. He began telling the boy that the monsters he saw were representations of Islam's enemies, that he had to go out and confront the monsters and kill them. It was a brilliant, if diabolical, use of mental illness in the service of jihad. So the family's fear was not only that the young man would be killed in Iraq, but that he wouldn't be able to get the medicine he needed and would fall into a schizophrenic decline.

The jihadi's brother, a lawyer in his late twenties, volunteered to go to Iraq with me. I was willing to try. My motto then was: If you ask me, and you're willing to do your part, I'll do what I can.

I met the brother in Amsterdam and then flew on to Istanbul, where we began planning to get the young man out. While I was working the case, the brother received a call from his father, who told him that he'd had a change of heart. He didn't want to risk a second son to save the first one; he forbade him to go to Iraq. The young man got off the phone, ashen-faced, and told me about the conversation. "You need to do it without me," he said.

I was furious. I'd come all this way and now he was abandoning the mission? This was his own brother we were talking about and he needed to be there to find him. It's not like calling Uber; you can't cancel at the last minute if you change your mind.

I really ripped into the guy, and he took it, shaking his head. "I know, I know," he said finally. "But I can't go against my father."

I almost called the operation off. I phoned the father and told him. "This wasn't the deal. I need your son to go with me to Iraq."

But the father was dead set against it. He could barely survive losing one son; two would be too much. He begged me to go ahead. "We trust you," he told me. I shouldn't have agreed, but the pain in the man's voice was clear. He couldn't sleep with the thought of ISIS taking both his sons, and I understood it. Grudgingly, I agreed to go on.

The boy had no Facebook account I could contact. I called my network and began sorting through pictures and videos on the Internet. I searched the more popular Twitter feeds and Instagram accounts for any mention of a South American fighter. Finally, after days of looking, I found a picture of him.

I flew alone to the north of Iraq. Kurdish territory. I stayed in a hotel in a town close to Mount Sinjar. The difference between Iraq and Syria hit me as soon as I walked out of the airport. I stared in amazement at the street scene: it seemed like every other car was a luxury model: Mercedes-Benz, BMWs, Ferraris, Range Rovers, Porsches. Syria felt like a country under siege; it was dry and dusty and the cars were beaten up, with cracked windshields, and even bullet holes, sometimes. Here there was wealth spread out before your eyes like some kind of smorgasbord. *Oil is a beautiful thing if you have it,* I thought. Investors were pouring into the Kurdish regions, American and British companies coming to provide services. In Syria, everyone was running the other way.

But there were ISIS operatives here, too, I knew. Every so often, a suicide bomber would detonate his explosives in a public place. It wasn't like you were in Miami or Berlin; it was more like Lebanon. Fun and wealthy, but with crazy things happening often enough to make you nervous.

Another thing I learned early on: Everyone here was an informant. Everyone here was providing information to this organization or that one. Your taxi driver was probably talking to the Kurdish intelligence service. The receptionist at your hotel might be cooperating with the police. All the hotels had cameras. The Kurds had been through enough in their long history not to trust anyone.

Before the rise of ISIS, Sinjar had been a Yazidi town, which made it a target for the caliphate's soldiers. Yazidis were particularly hated by the group; if you mentioned the sect to an ISIS fighter, their lips would curl down into a frown almost of disgust and they would tell you the most vicious slanders about these people.

This hatred led to a horrific massacre of five thousand Yazidi men in Sinjar. In August 2014, when ISIS attacked the town, the Kurdish *peshmerga* forces that were defending it had decided to leave, without telling the residents. They melted away in the middle of the night, leaving the population almost totally helpless before the advancing troops. ISIS came in and just laid waste to the place. They destroyed shrines, shot anyone who opposed them, and forced the Yazidis to pledge allegiance to the Islamic State or be killed.

Many townspeople fled to the nearby mountains. The images of these terrified people hiding in the crags and on the freezing slopes finally prompted the Americans and others to lead a relief effort, bombing the hell out of the ISIS positions. Those efforts saved tens of thousands of lives. But for five thousand men, it was too late. They'd already been murdered. That was the history I was wading into. It wasn't a good history. As the poet W. H. Auden once wrote:

I and the public know
What all schoolchildren learn,
Those to whom evil is done
Do evil in return.

This complicated the mission. The *peshmerga*, as I'd learned, were not sympathetic to young men who'd joined ISIS but had changed their minds. "Not sympathetic" is a euphemism; they were, in fact, happy to kill them. Many Kurds to whom I spoke before arriving in Iraq told me to forget about it. It was a waste of time. "If the *peshmerga* find your boy, they will kill him and they will kill the family member who came to find him, just because."

"That's what people told me when I first went to Syria," I replied. They had told me the FSA would shoot me. But instead, they'd helped me. You can't do this job without believing in people just a little bit.

For the West, the Kurds are the last remaining heroes left in the Middle East. They've been persecuted for decades and they're fighting ISIS on their own. I admire the *peshmerga*, too. Tough fighters, every inch the warriors that the most demented ISIS jihadis are. But I don't buy the entire myth. The Kurds torture prisoners, they put bodies behind trucks and drag them, they have their own problems with corruption. Yes, compared to ISIS, they're angels. But they're not lily white.

When we landed, I made contact with some Kurdish military officials. I stressed that my "client" suffered from a mental illness, and that the radicals had capitalized on this fact. You couldn't blame him for being ill. "If you find him," I asked, "what will you do? Will you torture him or will you bring him to me?" My contacts assured me that there would be no torture.

Were they lying to me? Was I leading this young man to freedom or was I cooperating in something that would leave him maimed or dead? I knew the *peshmerga* were merciless with other ISIS captives. Would they make an exception for this boy just because he was from the West?

Trust us, the *peshmerga* said. I had no other choice.

Then there was the problem of dealing with the young man himself. The boy's schizophrenia meant he couldn't be approached by someone saying, "Your brother sent me, he wants you to leave Iraq." This guy trusted almost no one, especially not strangers. And we knew he was off his medicines; there was no way that the Islamic State stocked that kind of specialized stuff.

I found more pictures online and saw who the Peruvian was with: Chechens and others from the territories of the former Soviet Union. I asked some Kurdish friends to make contact with his emir. They did so but the man refused to let the Peruvian talk to me. He wasn't going to give us the chance to persuade the guy to leave.

I didn't have the same network in Iraq that I did in Syria; I had to search around until I found an activist willing to go meet with the boy. I can't say much about who I found or what they did, because the people involved asked me not to, but my contacts got in touch with the Peruvian and eventually met with him. The boy knew he was sick; he was suffering hallucinations and hearing voices in his head. It didn't take that much convincing to get him to agree to leave. I think even he realized that he needed his medicine and would spiral into a dark place if he didn't get it.

My contacts smuggled him out of his battalion's camp and the *peshmerga* took control of him. They kept their word and didn't harm him in any way. But they did question him. For a solid month, the Peruvian was unable to leave. Finally, he was released and he crossed into Turkey and went almost immediately to the Istanbul airport and from there flew to Peru.

I was relieved and the family was ecstatic. The father called me to thank me, his voice breaking. I was so happy it had worked out.

Ironically, if you ask the son today about Iraq, he barely remembers it. He was in such a state of mental disorientation that he has only a few fragmented memories of that time. Perhaps that's for the best.

But I was also frightened by the Peruvian case. *How far will this epidemic spread?* I wondered. Would I soon be getting calls from Chileans, Japanese, Indonesians, families from Monaco and Hungary? The scope of the problem was mind-boggling, and I dreaded becoming a point man for desperate families around the world. I thought again about quitting.

Many people accused me of being a kind of human trafficker, of making money off these missions. But that's wrong; I never charged the families a cent. They paid all the expenses—my airplane tickets, my hotel, my food, my cigarettes. To be honest, at this time I was broke and had mounting debts I had no way of paying. Many months of working on my son's case and the missions for other families had left me no time to restart my career.

Maybe I thought about charging the families for a minute or two at the beginning, but it was impossible. I'd been through the same tragedy as them. How could I put a price on that, say, "You need to give me five thousand dollars or I can't help you"? That would have been immoral.

One time, a Saudi family contacted me and offered a nice amount of money for me to go to Syria and get their son, alone. I was surprised. An Arab family saying this? They knew the culture, they knew that a family member had to be right next to me for the deal to work. They didn't want to go, because they were afraid. But I said, "I'm sorry, I don't work like that."

I did pay my contacts inside Syria, the drivers and the go-betweens. How could I send them into Raqqa, the lion's mouth, without offering them some compensation? So money did change hands, but only two or three hundred dollars at a time. The risks they took for the money were serious. A few of my guys refused any cash; they did it because they believed in the mission. But I knew of other "fixers" who would charge ten times the price as my guys—three thousand dollars—to go into Syria and look for a fighter.

Chapter Twenty-Five

I WAS TALKING WITH HELEN one day in June 2015 when I felt my cell phone shudder. Texts. I didn't have time to look right away. When I finally finished with the call and looked at my messages, this is what I saw:

"Hello, I am a 16 year old American and my brother left for Syria last week. I heard about your story and I would like to contact you for help. Thank you for your time. . . .

"I guess we would like to talk to you for ideas. . . .

"Please help us."

I called the number and spoke to the boy's mother. She was emotional, sick with dread. It's always harder for the mother, I've found. The family lived in Virginia and their son had been recruited at school before leaving for Syria. The mom was Kurdish and the father was Shiite; the boy had been raised in the Shiite faith. That rang a warning bell. ISIS is Sunni, and they hate the Shiites. Why the hell had he gone to them?

I asked all the questions: *Why, how, where?* Same profile,

same modus operandi as my son. The father worked with cars and the mother was a teacher. Just an ordinary middle-class American family until all this happened. "This is not my son," she told me. "I don't recognize this person."

"What is he telling you?" I said.

"He insisted we stay where we are, that we not come to Syria," she told me. "You are a *kafir*," he said to her, an unbeliever, "so stay in your *kafir* country." This was how he was talking to his own mother. The young man had converted to the Sunni faith and said he'd been fully accepted by ISIS.

I didn't believe it. A Shiite who "converts" to Sunni isn't a full citizen in the caliphate. There's always doubt about his intentions. He is a half-person. This boy was being led down the garden path.

I went into my spiel. "It's possible to get him, but you need to be there, you need to come to the border with me." I had it memorized by now.

"But the FBI told us not to go to the border," the woman said. "It's too dangerous." This was frustrating; the FBI had never been to the border to try and get someone out. I had, many times. So why were they advising against the idea and offering nothing in its place?

We spoke for hours. The father agreed to meet me in Iraq. I booked my ticket and tried to get some sleep.

I met the father in the airport; he was overjoyed to see me. I recognized the signs: he was relieved to be finally doing something. A man is soothed by taking action.

I knew the son had gone through an international house and

taken his training. He'd been in Raqqa. But he'd disappeared after that. None of my contacts could get a fix on him. Bad news.

I told the family to talk to the Arab media. Their reporters were out in the field where the fighters were. An American joining ISIS wasn't a story you saw every day, so maybe they would assign a journalist to track him down. But the parents were hesitant; they were ashamed, I think, of what had happened and didn't want to broadcast it.

In desperation, I turned to a kind of fixer. This man was an Iraqi, a man with deep contacts inside ISIS. I knew he'd had success before with Yazidi captives. He'd negotiated with the Islamic State and gotten thirty of them released. He told people he did it as a charitable act, but I knew money had exchanged hands and suspected some of it had ended up in his pockets. He was an enigma. I wondered how he'd developed such excellent contacts inside ISIS. The thing was, I didn't know which side he was on.

We met him at a café in Aleppo. He was chubby, with rimless glasses and a round face. He looked like a prosperous lawyer; well dressed, his pants pressed and pleated. An operator. His English was very good.

He told the father and me that it was no problem for him to pass into ISIS areas. "No one at the checkpoints stops me," he said. If the American was in a prison, he could pay someone to get him out. It would take time, because there were so many secret prisons, each one controlled by a different fighting group. Sometimes the emirs would deny that these jails even existed;

or if they did admit that they existed, would deny that a certain person was being held there. I knew from Jay's case that this was true. The battalions wanted to present the illusion that everything was harmonious inside their operations. But it wasn't.

If the American wasn't in a prison, the fixer told us, he couldn't help us. "Find out more and get back to me," he said.

I called Abu Harb from the Free Lawyers of Aleppo, my number-one fixer. "This guy has disappeared off the map," I told him. "We have to find him."

Abu Harb said he would make a few calls. The next day, he got back to me: the American was in a hospital in Raqqa, with a broken right leg and a bullet wound to the foot. He'd been fighting against forces from Iran when he'd been wounded.

In the foot, I thought. That's a hard spot to get hit in battle. In my experience, whenever a soldier is wounded in the foot, it means only one thing: they shot themselves to get out of fighting.

The father and I were practically dancing a jig. Hospitals were better than prisons. And the fact that he'd shot himself in the foot, as we believed, meant that he was sick of ISIS, sick of Syria, sick of the whole game.

I call Abu Harb back. He found out the name of the American's emir and got him on the phone. The young man was wounded, he told the man, and the family wanted to get him good care in Turkey. Everything was ready: we'd arranged with the leader of a fighting group on the border with Turkey, who promised to help get the boy out if we could get him close. Would the emir release him?

Not a chance. The American stayed. Abu Harb relayed the bad news to me.

So we would have to look at getting the young man out without his emir's permission. I sent some of my men there to evaluate the hospital the jihadi was in. It was a fortress. The place was surrounded by armed guards who carried AKs and wore grenades. No one was being rescued from there without a squadron of heavily armed fighters, which we didn't have.

Things were heating up. The boy's mother flew to Iraq. We couldn't keep her away.

She called her son while I listened on speakerphone. "We have a spot for you waiting at a good clinic," she said. "Will you go?"

The boy's voice came through the speaker. *You're a kafir and no, I'm not coming to see you. This is a trick.* He told her to change her religion or she would die as an infidel. I wanted to take the phone and scream at the little bastard.

We improvised. The parents told me that the boy was close to his sister, the one who'd texted me originally. My brain began to hum. What if the girl suddenly became ill and was admitted to a hospital? What if she sent pictures to the jihadi, saying she wasn't doing well and wanted to see him?

The parents agreed and the family arranged everything. Two days later, some pictures arrived on the mother's phone: The girl, looking pale, her hair pasted to her forehead, lying in a hospital cot with an IV attached to her arm. It looked real.

We sent them to the son. His response? *I don't care about her.* Sometimes you just wonder if these people are really worth the trouble. I felt more like shooting the guy than rescuing him. ISIS had turned him into a hateful thing. I felt nothing for the boy, only for his family.

Love hadn't worked, so we tried sex. The jihadi had a girl-friend back in America. Now she began texting him saying that she wanted to come to Turkey and meet him at the border. She couldn't be away from him any longer. The son was single and wasn't having sex. She didn't *explicitly* say that was the purpose of her visit, but what young man would discount the possibility?

We waited to hear his response. The day after our little plot went into motion, the girlfriend texted us. "He insulted me," the girl said. "He called me all kinds of names and told me to stay home."

Damn it. The hooks were in deep.

I called Abu Harb. Would he go see the American himself? "Sure," he said.

Perfect. Abu Harb would go to the hospital, keeping his cell phone in his hand, open on a call to me. That meant we'd be able to hear everything.

Meanwhile, the man who'd recruited the boy in Virginia had been in touch with the American. The recruiter said he was under surveillance because the family had reported the matter to the police. The boy erupted. "If he's arrested," he texted his mother, "I'm going to strap on a suicide bomb and blow myself up." Later, the father went on an undercover mission for the FBI; he wore a wire to implicate the recruiter. But we kept that a se-cret. The boy obviously saw this brainwasher as a hero, so we tried to keep him out of the picture as much as possible.

The next day, Abu Harb set out for the hospital, with us listening in. "I've parked the car, approaching the entrance," he said. "There are fighters everywhere. No one has checked my ID."

We could hear the sound of his feet on the steps. There were voices in the background, but normal voices. No shouting.

I could hear Abu Harb's breathing.

"Going to the ward."

More steps. Then rapid-fire talk in Arabic. There was something going on. Abu Harb's voice was calm but urgent.

"Who is this he's talking to?" said the father.

"I don't know."

The mother's face looked strained. Her eyes searched mine.

Abu Harb came back on the phone. "It was a nurse," he said. "I told her I need to see the American. She won't be a problem."

Steps. Abu Harb asked someone a question in Arabic. An indistinct answer.

"What is he doing?"

I held my finger to my lips.

Finally, I heard Abu Harb.

"My friend, I've come to see you." He was talking to the American.

"Who are you?" a voice said. The mother gripped the father's hand and pulled it toward her. It was their son.

Abu Harb told the boy that his family had sent him to make sure he was OK.

"I don't know you," the young man said.

"Your family is very worried. Go to the clinic and get well. Then you can make your decision."

"If I come with you, I'll end up in an American prison." The boy's voice was bristling with anger. I felt my heart sink.

"No, no," Abu Harb said. "We'll make sure before you go back that there will be no—"

"Get out! Get out of here!" The boy was shouting at Abu Harb. Insults followed, only half of which I understood.

Abu Harb pleaded with the boy to listen. He told him he would die in Iraq and that he could do more for his brethren at home. But the boy was shouting at him to leave. This was extremely dangerous; if one of the guards heard the yelling and investigated, Abu Harb could end up in a prison, or worse.

Abu Harb's voice came through the phone. "I'm leaving. This isn't going to work."

The call was cut off. The mother and the father began to cry softly next to me. I felt awful; I had no answers for them. The boy trusted no one, not even an emissary sent by his parents.

After this, the mission began to fall apart. The parents wouldn't leave without seeing their boy. I took them to Reyhanli, at the border, to see if I could get them across. There we met a sheikh from al-Nusra who said he would take the mother into Syria and help her find her son. But something about him gave me a bad vibe. I told her I didn't trust him.

The parents were frustrated with me. Nothing was working and naturally you look for someone to blame. They began talking to other people in Reyhanli, looking for a miracle.

Finally, the mother found a local to take her into Syria. I wished her good luck and booked my ticket back to Belgium. There was nothing else I could do. She was like a cancer sufferer who's exhausted all the normal treatments and wants to go to a shaman for a miracle cure. I wished them all the luck in the world, but I'd taken them as far as I could.

Later I heard there were complications inside Syria, the nature of which I never discovered. The mother was unable to see her son. I suspect the boy resisted the meeting. He knew she was in Syria but wouldn't come to her or allow her to come to him.

Another tragedy. Another life gone.

Chapter Twenty-Six

I FELT LIKE MY LIFE was flying apart. I was in a strange little place of my own. I'd gotten half-famous by risking my life. I was helping families, which gave me the greatest satisfaction in my life. But there were too many of them; I felt tired in my soul.

People tell me, "You have PTSD." Not true. I don't wake up in the night in a cold sweat, thinking about having the barrel of an AK-47 put in my mouth. I just don't. Maybe it was my military experience, or maybe it was the fact that my mission was successful and I feel grateful rather than traumatized, but I'm not a "survivor" of anything.

I do have dreams about that basement in Kafr Hamra. The night after it happened, I dreamt that the extremists were throwing a hood over my face and beating me. But in this version, I fought back. I guess I wanted to be a little braver than I had been. And afterward, whenever I traveled in Syria and saw men with balaclavas, I immediately flashed back to that moment I got out of the car and walked into the villa. I had also developed a fear of basements. Every time I went into one, I could feel my palms grow clammy and my heart beating like a jackrabbit's.

But it's not PTSD like soldiers get. They've been through far worse than me. I would call it something else: ETTS. Exposure To Tragedy Syndrome. It was really seeing the pain in the faces of the parents that got to me.

An example: A Moroccan family came to see me. They'd lived in Belgium for years, the father in the metal industry, the mother a nurse. They'd made a life in their new country, had their own house, were still Muslims but not too serious about it; the father never wore a beard, for example. A good life in a city called Verveirs, which used to be a big textile center but now is a destination for tourists. A beautiful place to grow up. It was called the "Water Capital of Wallonia." How could anything bad happen in the Water Capital of Wallonia?

Easily. Their oldest son caught the bug. By now, you can probably guess the rest: a visit to a radical mosque (this one influenced by al-Shabaab, the "movement of striving youth" from East Africa) a change in clothes, a change in food, a new beard. Tell me when you've heard enough.

The same circle of radicals that got to the boy would later be broken up in a police raid. Two extremists were killed; they'd been talking to an ISIS ringleader in Greece and had been planning to execute police officers. His story was that he'd gone to

Verviers "to see his fiancée and was dropping off a pair of sneakers. He did not know that these guys were connected to international terrorism." When the police arrived, the man jumped out a window while his two friends picked up their guns before getting blown away by the cops.

This is what can happen in a small, out-of-the-way Belgian city. The Internet links everything to everything else.

So the family's eldest son disappeared one day. I went to see the family. The father was older than me, dressed in a leather jacket and jeans. Nice guy. He spoke for a few minutes before he began to cry.

I agreed to go to Iraq with the dad. I traced the boy's phone; the last usage had been in Anbar Province. Since then, nothing. We went to Iraq and the father felt better for being there. But we couldn't find a trace of the boy; nobody had heard anything. I had a feeling that he'd been dead for a while, because no one remembered the guy. That happens in places like Iraq, where fighting groups move from battle to battle, get broken up, lose members. When no one even remembers your name, you are really and truly dead.

I heard the conversations between the father and the mother back in Belgium, the same ones I'd had with Helen, but softer. "No, nothing. We will continue to look. I'm sorry, my love."

We went to Iraq twice, chasing leads. If only we could have found out what really happened to him, it would have eased the minds of the parents. But I could give them nothing, not even a fragment of his cell phone.

The parents are still looking. They're strong, they believe they will find their son. I wish them every good thing.

The problem was that there was a tragedy going on in Syria and Iraq that I was connected to, and that tragedy wasn't in the past. It was happening again every day, with fresh victims, fresh pain for fresh families. Nothing about it was history. I couldn't go three or four days without some request for help from a mother or a father. Do you think I'd listen to a mother crying on the phone and turn her away, block her number? What kind of a man does that?

But the constant traveling was wearing on me, and the tension of having people's lives balanced on my shoulders. If I made a wrong move, young men could die. And what if I helped bring back a fighter who then went on to blow up a shopping mall? Well, that was always in the realm of possibility. It was just . . . heavy.

What really weighed on me was that I felt like I was living the terror of losing Jay over and over again with these new families. The formula for how their sons got radicalized was so familiar to me, but no one was doing anything about it. There just wasn't anywhere else to turn for those lonely people who'd lost their children, and I began to feel overwhelmed. There needed to be some kind of agency, funded by Bill Gates or something, that did what I did. I was breaking down, drinking more, sleeping less. My wife, in *The New Yorker* article, said that I didn't drink water anymore, meaning I was on a whiskey-only diet. Not quite right; I had a soda once in a while, just for variety. You can't be on call twenty-four hours a day for desperate families if you're downing half a bottle of scotch a day. But she was right that this role of the jihadi hunter was messing up my life.

Meanwhile, back in Belgium, Jay was giving me little heart attacks. He'd met another girlfriend, one I didn't approve of. She had a criminal background and I thought she was a bad influence on my son. Together, they decided they were going to go on holiday to Turkey. This, of course, was forbidden by the terms of his parole. But he went anyway, and they were stopped at the airport. The intelligence services believed he was trying to go back to Syria to fight. But Jay told me it was just a vacation, a break. I chose to believe him.

If he ever does go back to Syria, there is no doubt in my mind he'll be killed. He's considered a traitor and someone that cooperated with the infidel police. I know that ISIS has lists of people they are looking to kill and I believe he's on one. I have no doubt that his old friends in Sharia4Belgium would celebrate his death and the extremists worldwide would join in, too. Because Jay was an insider; he saw what ISIS really was at its heart and he exposed it. They hate that.

I could see that Jay was still searching for his place in the world. He couldn't find a job because of his notoriety, and so he spent more and more time at home. He became obsessed with video games, especially the first-person-shooters that so many young men love. Perhaps this was a way to work off his frustration and anger at not being able to find work. He could track and kill the bad guys in the safety of his own room and feel just a tiny taste of the heroism that had eluded him in Syria.

Jay turned his new love into a little business. He spent so much time gaming, and became so good at it, that he actually helped with the beta testing of new releases. He found flaws in the software. The obvious benefit of this kind of work was that he could remain anonymous. Over e-mail, the company could never tell they were dealing with the notorious ex-jihadi Jejoen Bontinck. He was just a guy who loved gaming. He took comfort in that.

Jay took up horseback riding again. He went to the gym and trained until he was ready to drop. And he developed a mantra that he would tell himself over and over again when he faced another rejection, another curse from the crowd. "Persevere through trial and error. Winners are good losers." This is what he told himself to get through. And, thank God, it seemed to be working.

We spent many hours together talking about Syria. He was intrigued by my efforts to find him; he demanded I spell out every little detail of my trips. When I told him about my close calls, with the Libyan boy at the border between eastern and western Aleppo, for example, he would shake his head in amazement. "I can't believe that you went there!" he said, cackling with glee.

There was one moment that stuck with me. Jay told me that when he was in the Aleppo prison with James Foley and John Cantlie, they talked a lot about their families. Jay told them that he and I hadn't always seen eye-to-eye about Islam and other things. One afternoon, he revealed to the two Westerners that I'd come to Syria to look for him; other jihadis had told him that I'd gone around the country meeting with emirs and the most radical fighters, in the hopes of finding my son.

James and John were fascinated. "If you don't talk with your father, you're just pissing in the wind," they told Jay. And I think that was the moment when his heart began to change. He found that he was impressed by what I'd done; he was even proud of me.

One time, we'd talked about Kafr Hamra and my nasty encounter there and Jay stopped. "I'll never forget what you did," he said. "I want to say thank you." I could feel tears coming to my eyes; there was no need for any more words. I hugged him.

I had hopes for my son again, normal hopes. That he would to go back to school, study for a profession, begin a career. He began taking a business course to help people become entrepreneurs and scored an 88 on his final. For me, that was a victory. Jay was directing his mind toward new things.

What were my dreams for my son? An ordinary life. For him to open a restaurant or a kickboxing center, or some kind of little business, that would be a huge thing. I wanted him to be happy and at peace. What any parent wants, really.

But I couldn't stop worrying that he would slip back into the extremists' arms. That thought lay squatting at the back of my mind like some malevolent little reptile.

Chapter Twenty-Seven

AS I TRAVELED FROM THE West to the Middle East, I met so many kinds of men and women, each of them a cross section of the forces at work in places like Syria. Some of them were victims, and some were part of the breed who wanted only to help. One guy, Ahmad, was a bit of both. He did what I did, but paid an even more serious price. If you want to understand what Jay and I and so many other people went through, one of the best ways is to listen to Ahmad's story. There isn't another like it.

Ahmad Walid Rashidi was a Danish student who was hoping to become a doctor. Just twenty-two, he was in the middle of his studies at a medical school; his parents were Afghan and he'd made them proud by his hard work and excellent marks in school. He was on his way to joining the Danish upper class.

He'd gone through a great deal to reach this point in his life. At five years old, while living in Kabul, he was caught in the crossfire between two groups of rival fighters. A bomb shattered his leg. "I saw something green and metal, then everything turned black," he remembered. "I was then on the ground, in our garden, my face was on the earth, and there was huge smoke and glass was all around. I saw fire in the stone. I told myself, *Stones can't be on fire.*"

The doctors thought he was gone. "They put a white sheet on my body, and a voice said, 'He's dead.' I heard my mother and grandmother yelling, 'No, no, no!'" The sheet was removed and doctors managed to save him, though his damaged leg was amputated. He spent months in a local hospital, where aid workers for a charity found him. They arranged for a German hospital to give him the treatment and therapy he needed; Afghanistan had few facilities for amputees, especially children. The five-year-old Ahmad was taken in by a German family.

While he was away, the violence in Afghanistan notched higher. The Taliban killed both his father, because he was a Communist, and his older brother. The country was no longer a viable place for his family to live, so in the winter of 2000, his mother, a university lecturer in Kabul, traveled to Iran and then on to Denmark with the rest of the family. The family was accepted as legitimate refugees fleeing war and began their new lives in Copenhagen. Ahmad soon joined them.

Ahmad was fortunate. He had a new prosthetic, competent doctors, a free public school to attend, and a roof over his head. But life was still difficult: his disability made him a target. The young boy was mocked and pushed around by other, stronger students. He found Danish students were unsympathetic to Afghani suffering. "It built up resentment. People here in the

West gather around a dinner table to discuss the death of a pet, but no one asked me what happened to my leg."

Ahmad was well on his way to becoming a jihadi. "I was full of hate," he admits. The West didn't understand or care for him, at least in his own mind, and so he itched to destroy it.

He fought back. He fought with bullies, other students, even teachers. "I was basically a criminal," he said. When he was still a boy, it looked as though Ahmad was going to become a statistic: one of the refugees who doesn't fit in with his adopted society, becomes a bitter outcast, and turns extremist. But that's not what happened. Somehow, Ahmad had turned it around. He buckled down in school, left his criminal friends to their fates, and even started a charity called "Walking Future," which provided prosthetic limbs for victims of the violence in Afghanistan.

Then, one afternoon in June 2015, Ahmad's cell phone rang while he was walking through the Tivoli Gardens amusement park. It was a friend he'd known for years, and Ahmad knew why he was calling. Two twin sisters in Britain, related to his friend by blood, had recently disappeared into thin air. Perhaps because he'd suffered himself, Ahmad sympathized with the family's situation. He volunteered to help.

The family's bewilderment was well founded. The two Somali-British girls had been living in England for a decade and had seemed to take to the country like ducks to water. They were obsessed with clothes, with taking pictures of themselves and their friends, and going out. Normal British girls from just outside Manchester.

But earlier that month, their parents had knocked on their bedroom door and told the girls to get ready for school. No answer. When they pushed the door open, the parents were startled to find the girls' beds empty. Somehow, in the middle of the night, the pair had packed their bags, gone to the front door of their redbrick home, and walked out into the night.

The parents notified their extended family and everyone began searching for the twins. Bit by bit, they pieced together what had happened. The girls had snuck away to Turkey, intending to head to Syria and join ISIS. Without the parents having a clue, they'd been reading ISIS propaganda online and scanning the literature passed out by Salafist extremists in their hometown.

The girls had been cleverer than most boys. They didn't change their clothes or their eating habits. They didn't start talking about the persecution of the Muslims or the need for jihad. They'd just gone about their ordinary lives until one day they made the journey to the caliphate. They'd made it as far as Turkey.

Ahmad decided to try and bring the girls back before they ruined their lives forever. "I was not afraid of death," he said. He'd always believed that only truly good people died, as a relief from unbearable situations, such as his brother and father suffering under the Taliban. "I had nothing to lose."

Ahmad had no experience in the Middle East. But he had dark hair, dark eyes, and a beard and could easily pass for a Syrian or Iraqi. He was like me: a determined amateur. So he packed a small suitcase with clothes that seemed suitable for the hot temperatures of Syria, some toiletries, and face cream, and headed for the airport. He thought the whole trip would take a week.

He arrived in Hatay Airport in southern Turkey on June 28, 2015. The air was muggy and oppressive, very different from Copenhagen's cool breezes. Halay had been nicknamed "ISIS International Airport" because it was a main way station for European fighters on the journey to Syria. Ahmad was hopeful, but he'd yet to get a fix on the girls' intentions or even a vague idea of their location.

"I didn't know if they were in Turkey or Syria," he said. "But I knew that it would become increasingly difficult to save them, the longer time went by."

He headed to Reyhanli, my old haunt, because everything happened in Reyhanli. He rented a hotel room and began asking around about two British girls who'd gone over to ISIS. No luck. No one had heard anything, or more likely, no one was telling him anything. His Middle Eastern looks only went so far; in fact, with so many operatives and spies and double-dealing types around Reyhanli, they might have even hurt him.

Ahmad decided he had to take a risk. He slipped over the border into Syria. He wrote a note to a Danish friend outlining his progress:

I was over the Syrian border and back and found out that the girls have not yet gone into Syria—they are probably in Turkey. There are three major groups of rebels in Syria and I have spoken to two of them. I have not been able to talk to the last one, which is ISIS. ISIS is typically the one that seduces girls and once they have got into their clutches, there's not much that can be done.

For a beginner, Ahmad had learned quite a bit in a very short time. He was doing well. But in the next few days, he ran into the kind of shysters and opportunists that I'd had to wade through in Reyhanli. People who tell you they can get anyone out of Syria for the right price. Others who offered protection from ISIS kidnappers. It really is the Wild West and Ahmad was learning the first rule of such a place, which is that there are no rules.

On June 30, Ahmad arranged a meeting with an ISIS official. For this, he traveled to the large city of Sanliurfa in southeastern Turkey and found his contact waiting at a café. The young man, whose arms were bulging with muscles, didn't say he could find the girls but, like others in Reyhanli, told Ahmad that he would be in danger in Syria and that he could protect him.

Around this time, one of the sisters posted a photo on Instagram, along with a message:

Thanks to be God. . . . I am 16 and among the women warriors of Dawlat-al-Islam. I swear we travelled from England to Sham (Syria) in one day. God Is Great. I wish you all were here and see what I see. The city is unbelievably beautiful. The black banner is everywhere. Women who are fully covered and naturally a million flies that attack me constantly. If God wills it I'll soon have a good Internet connection as

I've taken a lot of pictures with my Ipad that I would like to share with you.

So the girls had made it to Syria after all, and at least one of them seemed happy to be there. Not good news for Ahmad.

The Danish man kept looking for contacts to get the girls out. He met a Turk from Antakya who offered to find the girls for five thousand dollars. His information was that the twins were in al-Bab, taking classes at a sharia school. After about a month of this instruction, they would leave the school and be free to marry. It was crucial to get to them before this happened.

This was when I heard from Ahmad for the first time. I met him in the Turkish city of Gaziantep. I was on another mission and our paths crossed. He told me his story, why he was in Syria and about his fears that if the two girls left the school and were married, they would be lost forever. And he asked for my help.

I said, "Of course I'll help you." I called around to my contacts. They'd heard of the girls and said the al-Bab story sounded plausible. Ahmad decided to go to al-Bab and see if he could meet the girls face-to-face. It was a highly dangerous thing to do. ISIS prizes its female recruits. To go to the sharia school and ask them to leave . . . well, it took balls.

On July 6, there was more news: ISIS announced on social media that the girls were going to wed two British-Afghan fighters. I heard from my sources that the report was accurate and that the weddings would happen within a few days.

Ahmad felt he had to move fast. "Once the twins were married there would be no turning back," he said. The same problems I faced with getting Laura Passoni out would be repeated, exacerbated by the fact that the girls were newly arrived in Syria and still enthralled by living in the caliphate. Their new husbands wouldn't let them leave the house and passes would be impossible to get.

Ahmad now found it necessary to bring a family member into the picture. He convinced the woman's mother to come to Turkey to help persuade the twins to leave. He began telling people that he was the woman's son-in-law, and he was helping her get her children back. It's funny how the experience of working in Syria and Iraq channels rescuers like us into the same methods; there are only a few things that really work. A single guy looking for two future jihadi brides? That was like nitroglycerin.

The twins' mother arrived in Turkey on July 20. "She said that she wouldn't be able to look at herself in the mirror without having tried to get her daughters back home again," Ahmad said. "She was very courageous." Now it was time to cross the border and head into Syria. Ahmad had his doubts. *"Afraid to be killed or forced into jihad,"* he messaged one of his Danish friends.

Ahmad gathered everything he'd need for a rescue mission— passport, money, clothes—and stuck them in two plastic bags. After nearly two weeks of preparation, Ahmad and the girls' mother were finally ready to cross. *"I haven't slept all night because of my excitement,"* Ahmad messaged to a friend. *"We're on our way to Syria."* He told one of his closest buddies that if they didn't hear back from them within eight days—the time he estimated he would need to travel to al-Bab, persuade the

girls to leave, formulate a plan to get them out, and execute it—
that they should let officials know that something had gone
wrong. He was being a bit optimistic. In my experience, there's
no way to judge how long a rescue will take. There are so many
variables in the equation it can make your head spin, and the
thing you least expect to go wrong is the one that always does.

A smuggler took Ahmad and the older woman across one of
the well-worn routes between Turkey and Syria. They were
headed for Manbij, in northeastern Syria. It was a predomi-
nantly Sunni city, which in ancient times was inhabited by a
religious sect that built huge phallic sculptures before their
temples; once a year, on a sacred day, believers climbed the phalli
and covered them with decorations. There were three hundred
priests who held ceremonies at the sect's shrine and practiced self-
mutilation as well as joining in the occasional orgy.

ISIS arrived in the city in January 2014, and turned it into a
center of the illegal trade in antiquities and stolen relics. It was
a crazy place. Other rebel groups, such as the Free Syrian Army,
were trying to steal Manbij away from the Islamic State, and
the jihadis had responded by setting off car bombs to defend
their bases. The city was also frequented by European fighters
who were on their way to the front lines. Ahmad thought this
gave him a good chance of finding someone who'd seen the twins.

Ahmad was startled by what he found in Manbij. There were
so many European jihadis in the city that they'd named it "Little
London." He heard English and German being spoken on
the streets. After settling in at his hotel, he began making

contacts. He called himself "Ahmad al-Afghani" (Ahmad the Afghan) and asked to meet with some Islamic State representatives. He scored an early success when an ISIS guy heard his story and invited him and his "mother-in-law" to sleep at his house.

Progress. He texted a friend: "*Quite satisfied with the situation. IS won't touch me because I'm civilian. And the civilians won't touch me because I'm IS. A real win-win situation.*"

But Ahmad was making mistakes. He told people in the town that he had plenty of money to get the girls out and hinted that he would pay anyone who could make it happen. The girls' family had sold a bunch of gold to pay for the mission. That only made him a target for opportunists.

The next day, he was asked to have dinner with some ISIS guys at their training base. He gladly accepted. But things began to sour quickly. One of Ahmad's contacts directed him to a house where he believed one of the twins had been staying with her British-Afghan fiancé. Ahmad rushed to the villa to see if the girl was still living there. When she wasn't, he made a scene.

"I got angry and frustrated and told the people in the front of the house that I would get the IS police involved so that we could see the girls." That's what Ahmad said afterward. What I heard was slightly different: I was told that when the girls weren't produced, he told the occupants of the house that he was going to hire someone to kidnap the twins and take them out of Syria.

Ahmad was a bit too cocky. To say that he was an "untouchable," as he messaged his friend, wasn't correct. No one is untouchable in ISIS territory except for its leaders. Even some of its own generals and emirs have found themselves in prison or in front of an executioner's gun because they disobeyed the laws of the caliphate. A stranger who just arrived in Syria the day before should never get too comfortable. And Ahmad did.

Here's where things got a bit weird. Ahmad had told people in Turkey that he was the son-in-law of the girls' mother. But my sources told me that in Syria, he'd come up with another cover story: that he wanted to marry one of the girls. That might have hurt him, too. Because those girls were promised to ISIS jihadis, and he'd just become their competition. They had guns and connections. He didn't.

The police were headquartered in a former movie theater. Ahmad brought the twins' mother in and began to talk with the officials there. To his surprise, the Islamic State representatives knew quite a bit about him and the older woman. They announced that the girls' mother had given an interview to a Western television channel and denounced ISIS for taking her daughters. As for Ahmad, he was condemned as a journalist and a spy.

This was much worse than merely insulting the occupants of the home he'd just visited. Later, Ahmad found out the source of these charges: the husband of one of the girls.

The twins' mother was taken away to a female prison and Ahmad was ushered into the male wing. He was searched and all his possessions were bagged: his wallet, his money, his passport and some face cream, and his cell phone. (His friends noticed that after August 4, there were no more messages from Ahmad.) He'd taken the precaution of putting his student ID card, the mother's credit cards, and some other valuable things into his prosthetic leg.

One of my contacts phoned me soon after this happened and explained to me what had gone down. I called Ahmad's family and told them that he'd been detained. They were distraught.

It was a forbidding place, that prison. There were men wearing balaclavas walking around carrying AK-47s. I know what Ahmad was feeling at that moment: the sensation of having entered a different realm. But he remained calm. He thought that he'd be able to prove that the charges against him were false and that he'd soon be released to resume his mission.

The guards now took Ahmad to his jail cell. It was unbearably crowded, mostly with young men accused of small-time crimes, and ISIS fighters who'd done something bad: refused to carry out an order or left their camp without permission. There were all kinds of people mashed together, shoulder to shoulder.

"There were so many people sitting in there that they couldn't even stretch their legs. You had to sit there with your knees up in a sort of fetal position on the cement floor. One of the other prisons had been bombed so IS said that they had to move some of the prisoners over to the prison I was at."

A fetid smell hung in the air. The only toilet for the dozens of men was located in the cell itself. But these were inconveniences and represented no true danger to Ahmad. Talking was forbidden. What really worried Ahmad were the men in the balaclavas, the guards. They not only wanted to look sinister; some of them actually were.

Ahmad had grown used to Danish ways, and so he expected to have his case heard quickly and decided in his favor. But this was Syria, and things were different.

Soon after he settled himself onto the cement floor of the cell, he heard screaming. Someone was being hurt close by.

Every so often, a guard would come for a prisoner. There was no warning. "One of the prisoners had spoken aloud, and at one point the guards came, grabbed him round his neck, and pulled him out of the cell. We could hear them beating him and he didn't come back again until a couple of hours later."

Ahmad's turn came after a couple of days. Guards came to take him out of the cell into a small area paved with stone. "They hit me and I fell down. Then they began to kick me. I didn't resist, as that would simply make it worse. I covered my face and hoped that it would soon end. It was a question of not beginning to cry or anything. I could see from the other prisoners that the ones who seemed most afraid were the ones who got beaten the most."

This is the ISIS way. Beat first, and then ask questions. Perhaps they are so violent and numb in their own selves that they think that the only way to get the truth is through smacking the hell out of someone. Ahmad found this out quickly.

He was returned to the cell. His body ached. No reason had been given for the beating but, as the days went by, Ahmad made his own judgment: Those suspected of being anything other than devoted Muslims got the short end of the stick. And those suspected of doing things for the West—either espionage or plain old reporting—were doubly cursed. The penalty for spying was clear. "I was told that if the accusations against us were true, both the mother and I would be decapitated."

Ahmad was taken to another prison, the first of several moves he would make during his captivity. This is a common tactic for

ISIS, both to confuse their prisoners and to keep them away from any potential rescuers. The new place was in the mountains and here Ahmad had more space to move around. When he paced off the new cell, he found it to be eight footsteps by fifteen footsteps.

Ahmad began to play-act for his captors: he studied the Koran, prayed five times a day, and promised that, if he were released, he would condemn European countries for their behavior in Syria. If he was hoping to win favor, he failed. The beatings became more intense. At various times, Ahmad could hear men being tortured in the prison basement, while the guards yelled, "Allahu Akbar!"

Executions were a frequent thing. "After prayers they came in and took some of the prisoners out. I didn't always know what the prisoners had done, but they were pulled out in front and there was this sound of shots or of people having their heads cut off. It was terrible." One elderly prisoner went around the cell embracing his fellow inmates before he, too, was taken out and killed. The inmates figured out a method to determine what had happened to other prisoners. If they heard the guards shout, "*Takbir!*" ("Remember!") and that wasn't followed by gunfire or the sound of a car's engine, indicating the prisoner was being driven to another prison, that meant the inmate had been beheaded.

The stress wore on Ahmad. He needed to show he was unbowed, so he began refusing meals, to demonstrate that he was still in command of his own destiny. "I used that as a way to make my mark—to show that I was strong and independent." He was asked again and again to confess to espionage, but he refused. When the guards gave him a small notebook to write out his crimes, he used it instead to pen a farewell letter to his loved ones.

After more than a month of imprisonment, the girls' mother was released from the woman's prison. Ahmad had been moved again. The new jail was better, and he was beginning to form connections with his guards. He wrote a letter to his family saying he had enlisted with ISIS voluntarily.

Ahmad was brought to see an ISIS leader, an English jihadi. It was a fortunate meeting for him. "We had a good connection. We were like high school classmates, joking, talking. We were testosterone bombs." He also started giving medical advice to some of the guards. He examined other prisoners and evaluated their condition as best he could. All of this earned him better treatment. He tried to use what little influence he had to soften the prisoners' treatment. He persuaded the ISIS men that the captives would respond better to verbal orders than to beatings.

But some of what he did wasn't so noble. When other inmates were beaten, he said nothing and did nothing. And he even imitated the guards in small ways, like tossing a pan of cold water on dozing inmates to show that he wasn't one of them but was instead allied with their captors. "I was not happy with it," he said, "but it had to be done."

As much as he tried to hold himself apart from his situation, he began to sympathize with his captors. The more Ahmad talked with the young men of the Islamic State, the more he found their arguments persuasive. "They are like . . . what do you call them? Mermaids. They just sing, day to day, and I listen."

The British jihadi arranged a hearing of Ahmad's case. He went to the sharia court. "We were called into a sort of interrogation and I said several times that if the Islamic State found proof for what we had been accused of, I accepted being decapitated. But that I knew that I was innocent."

The jurists withdrew to decide his fate. After waiting anxiously for the verdict, Ahmad was told that his case had been dismissed for lack of evidence. He was freed and even given a pass that allowed him to travel through the caliphate's checkpoints. It was a total victory, but it had taken away months of his life and delayed the search for the two girls.

Ahmad was able to arrange a meeting between the two girls and their mother. They even spent an evening together catching up and talking about the future. But the twins were insistent: they wanted to remain in the caliphate.

It was crushing news for Ahmad and the family. All that effort, all that agony, and the girls refused to listen to them.

The mother and Ahmad took a bus to the town of Jarabulus. From there, they took another to the Turkish border. "Darkness fell," Ahmad remembered, "and at the border we had to wait half an hour to see if there were police on the other side. Finally, we crossed the border in groups of four. On the other side, there were two white delivery vans without lights and with their engines switched off." The pair boarded one of the vans and were driven to the Turkish town of Gaziantep. They had to go to the Danish embassy in Ankara and ask for money for airplane tickets back home. Embassy officials agreed and the pair arrived back at Copenhagen Airport.

Ahmad resumed his life in Denmark. The twins stayed in Syria. But for Ahmad, the bitter memories he carries from his rescue mission are centered on his friend, the British ISIS official who helped him get out. "I betrayed him," he said. "Let me ask you, how can I fight these guys when I've left half my heart in Syria?"

It's fascinating to me that this young man, whose father and brother had been killed by Taliban extremists and who saw first-hand the cruelty of the caliphate's soldiers, could still be vulnerable to their message. If anyone should have been steeled against ISIS propaganda, it should have been Ahmad. But he listened, and he was moved.

It was the claim that ISIS was fighting the humiliation of Muslims by the West that struck Ahmad the hardest. It rekindled his own memories of being a refugee child in Denmark, his grievous wounds ignored (or so he felt) by his fellow students. It was as if Muslims were second-class citizens and ISIS was the only one fighting their victimization. To me, it sounds crazy— Denmark opened its arms to Ahmad and his family, gave them freedom and food and shelter. To repay them with bitterness—I don't understand it. But for Ahmad, and so many other young men, the low status of Arab countries in the world is deeply felt. ISIS made "the West get a taste of its own medicine." Ahmad came close to being one of their true believers. He now calls himself and others like him "ticking bombs . . . bombs which are huge and which will one day explode."

Chapter Twenty-Eight

IN THE FALL OF 2015, a new kind of opportunity arose for me. Two female BBC journalists wanted to make a documentary about the antiquities and precious art that ISIS was stealing from museums and other sites and selling to fund their insurgency. It would be a twist for me: instead of helping people, I would try to save the physical objects that carried within them the ancient culture of Syria. And I would, for once, be paid for my work.

The world believed that the Islamic State was in the business of destroying ancient monuments with jackhammers and bulldozers. This was true. They videotaped their soldiers smashing a two-thousand-year-old statue of a lion from a Palmyra museum; they destroyed a thirteenth-century tomb in the city of Kirkuk in northern Iraq. They intercepted smugglers who were taking precious artifacts out of the countries and flogged them, then demolished the statues. They wrecked a museum in Mosul and laid waste to archeological sites in places like Nimrud and Hatra,

Iraq. Often, they would use dynamite and heavy equipment in their rampages.

ISIS looks at these treasures as vestiges of idol worship forbidden by the Koran. They claim that the artifacts are evidence of *shirk* (polytheism) and that they are establishing *tawhid* (monotheism), as Allah directs. But there is more to it. Not only do these actions enrage Westerners, they also send the message that ISIS is clearing the landscape of previous civilizations so that it can establish the one true caliphate. Wiping the slate clean.

But these journalists had come across some fascinating information. ISIS wasn't just destroying these artifacts; they were selling some of the smaller ones. Why? To add millions of dollars to their treasuries in order to keep fighting their enemies. In fact, the theft had become organized, complete with licenses issued by a department of "precious resources" allowing people to excavate the ruins at historical sites and extract the valuable artifacts. One French group that studied such issues estimated that the Islamic State controlled no less than 4,500 ancient sites, and was pillaging many of them for things to sell.

The BBC journalists wanted to expose this illegal trade and they asked me to go along as an advisor to the documentary. I was happy to do it. Finally, I would be able to use my expertise for a job that didn't involve terrified fathers and weeping mothers. I needed a break from bad emotions.

We traveled to Turkey and made our way to the Syrian border, where many of these artifacts were being smuggled. It was thrilling; we were meeting with smugglers and buyers, taping some of them on secret video. It was going to be a big story, and I was excited to be part of it.

We'd gotten about half of the footage we needed to complete the film when one day we were stopped on the street by Turkish antiterror police. I knew immediately we were in trouble. They'd obviously been tracking us for some time to know where we were going to be that day. And since we were going to meet a smuggler, I was wearing an undercover camera to film the encounter. I knew that Turks were paranoid about Western spies. Not good.

The police grabbed us all at once. "We are journalists," I said, "be careful what you do." They hustled us into cars and drove us to the headquarters of the antiterror squad. They brought in two interrogators. They knew who I was from my past exploits. I tried to explain that we were journalists working on a project; we had all the proper documentation. But all the police wanted to know was about ISIS. Were we working with them? Spying for them, perhaps?

I got a strange feeling from the Turkish interrogators. They kept returning to questions about Jay: How did I get him out? Who helped me? They seemed obsessed with that case and I sensed that they didn't really believe that I'd gone in to Syria alone and gotten my son out. For them, that was a million-to-one shot, so there must be something else at work in my story. Maybe they, too, believed I was working for an intelligence service. I told them the basic story, but didn't give any extra details. No way would I provide the names of the guys who'd helped me.

They searched me and found two cell phones. Those things were lifelines. They had the names of dozens and dozens of contacts I'd used to rescue Western fighters, as well as pictures and videos. They confiscated them. "I need those back," I told one of the officers. He nodded and said nothing.

They found the camera, and now they got really excited. "Why are you wearing this? Are you filming Turkish places—military, police?"

I told them I needed a lawyer and a translator before I'd answer any of their questions. I didn't want to "confess" to something because the interrogators couldn't—or didn't want to—understand my answers. After a long wait, an older, rumpled man entered the room and began to translate.

They asked again if I was filming Turkish places. "No," I said. "I'm trying to catch smugglers and ISIS operatives taking precious artifacts out of Syria. That's all."

I was so focused on proving I wasn't a spy that I failed to look at the documentary through Turkish eyes. Revealing to the world that the country was letting invaluable statues and other things flow across their borders and disappear into the hands of private collectors, perhaps never to be seen again, would be a black eye for the country. Another stick to beat Turkey with: *Not only are you letting jihadis cross your border, you're helping ISIS finance its war.*

I was too outraged to understand this. The police knew who I was. Why on earth would I go to work for ISIS after they stole my son away from me? The group represented everything I thought to be evil in the world.

No matter. I stood up and marched to another office. There, a doctor inspected me. I felt my spirits sink. Why would they be doing this, I thought, if they thought we would be leaving soon? This is something you do when a person is being admitted to a prison for a long time.

After my examination, guards marched us into the basement of the interrogation center. I felt the memories of my beating in Syria return; the fear, the sweating. I was terrified to walk down those stairs and shouted for the guards to stop, but they pulled me along. They threw me in a small, dimly lit cell and put the two BBC journalists in one opposite me. *I'm a prisoner again,* I thought to myself. I listened for the footsteps of the guards. I felt sure they would come back and start beating me.

Suddenly, the lights went off. I was sitting in complete darkness. I was overcome with a feeling of suffocation: My throat seemed to be closing up, I couldn't get enough air.

The electricity came back on. After that, it never went off. There was a light above my head and the guards refused to shut it off to allow me to sleep. There was no bathroom, not even a bucket. When I needed to use the facilities, I called out to the guards. They ignored me. I began banging on the steel door. No answer. It took ages for them to finally open the door and escort me to a bathroom that was unimaginably dirty.

I asked to call my embassy. The guards just shook their heads.

It was deliberate humiliation. They gave us no food and no water. I was pissed off and began yelling to the guards: "This is why you'll never become part of the EU. We are journalists and you're treating us like animals!" I banged on the door some more.

The miserable night passed slowly. The cell was freezing and filthy. I lay on my cot and thought of spending a few years in prison. This detention center would be paradise compared to a Turkish jail, especially as a Western prisoner.

The questioning and the mistreatment resumed the next morning. Then the officials told us we were leaving. That same day, we were released and put on a flight for Greece. The officials told us, "Don't come back." I felt relief flood over me. It was too good to be true.

I was in Athens for two days before flying on to Belgium, where we were questioned again. The Belgian authorities looked into the matter and agreed that we were in the right. I bought a new phone and called my lawyer. "We are free, Kris! They've let us go." The BBC had hired a Turkish lawyer to help get us out, and he was key to our release.

The experience left a bitter taste in my mouth. I'd been trying to help but had been treated like a criminal. Plus, I had the feeling that Turkish intelligence was now watching me anytime I entered the country and would harass me at every turn. Maybe they didn't like the attention I was bringing to their porous border, where ISIS operatives went back and forth as though they were going to Disney World.

Turkey is done for me, I thought. The next time, they won't be so understanding. And if Turkey was done, then my days of going personally to the border to get people out was over, too. Turkey was the conduit, and I couldn't operate without it.

I felt a sense of sadness admitting this to myself. I knew I would still help the families. I could never turn away a parent who came to me as a last resort. I still had my contacts inside Syria and my journalist friends. Yusuf was a phone call away and I knew he would help me whenever he could. Abu Harb was still in Aleppo, still doing the good work of the Free Lawyers of Aleppo. I would put the desperate mothers and fathers in touch with them and strategize about how to get their sons and daughters out of the maelstrom.

I wouldn't, however, go back to Syria. I knew it was the right thing to do for my health, both mental and physical. But when a place has filled such a colorful chapter in your life, has tested you in ways that you always feared to be tested, you can't forget it. I will never forget the smells and tastes of Syria, and the sounds—the incredible mix of street Arabic, of honking horns, of the *thunk* of mortars punctuating a bright morning. The call to prayers and the great, hushed silence that follows it.

I won't forget what it gave me back: Jay. Nor how it made me feel so alive that to wake up, bleary-eyed and with a sore back after a night spent lying on a concrete floor, was still a gift.

Epilogue

ON A SUMMER AFTERNOON IN 2015, months after the Sharia4Belgium trial had ended, Jay called me and asked me to take a walk with him. I agreed and we strolled through Antwerp, enjoying the hot weather. I noticed that he was carrying something in a plastic bag. It was good to be with him, like in the old days, walking without the threat of prison or suicide missions or ISIS assassins in our minds.

We found ourselves crossing a bridge over the River Scheldt. Jay stopped and looked over the railing, and I joined him. The cold water beneath us was flowing toward the North Sea.

He reached for the bag and took out two garments; I recognized them as djebellas he'd worn in Syria and afterward. I was surprised and a little spooked to see those things. They carried bad vibes for me, but I said nothing. Jay looked down at the water, deep in thought. Then he lifted the djebellas and threw them into the river.

"I've had enough of it," he said. We watched the garments

floating on the water's surface, heading toward the sea. And then we resumed our walk.

It was like a cleansing. He'd thrown off the remnants of a life he no longer had any use for. The indoctrination was over; he felt free inside himself and he wanted to get rid of the outer symbols of that horrible time. I was overjoyed to hear it, and to have witnessed the final, ritual act that put an end to his life as an extremist.

Today, if you met Jay you would see a young man in his early twenties who is smart, happy, and still looking for what he wants to do in his life. I'm so happy for him and so grateful that he is embarked on this new chapter in his life.

I know I'm not the only reason Jay is alive and free. One of my dreams is that I will soon be gathered with all the people who helped me rescue him. In the dream, we're in an apartment or a hotel room in Aleppo and we're seeing each other for the first time in years. Jay is there, and together we go through the room, shaking hands and embracing the guests one by one. There are no explosions in the distance; peace has come to Syria. It's a wonderful dream. I hope to live to see it.

I don't miss Syria but I miss its people. Its generous and large-hearted people. I miss you even as I write these words.

In writing this memoir, I've realized how many dark things I've been through. Some of them I had forgotten, or at least pushed to the back of my mind. I relived things I'd never expected to think of again and, honestly, many of the memories are wrenching. I was swept back up in the emotions I experienced in Syria and Iraq, and adrenaline surged into my veins. I saw the faces of people whom I'd tried to save and who are now gone. I saw the faces and felt the touch of the hands of their parents. Writing a memoir is like therapy, but the notes end up in public.

In November, word came from Syria that Brian De Mulder, the former soccer star who'd run away to ISIS, had been killed in a bombing. Pictures of his body appeared on the Internet; blood speckled his face, more of it on the pillow his head rested on. "He is now in paradise," announced the jihadi bride he'd married in Syria.

I called his mother, Ozana, to see how she was taking the news. She told me she didn't believe the reports. It appeared to be Brian in the photos, but she couldn't be sure. In a way, it would have been easier for Ozana if she could be sure that Brian was dead and no longer suffering. "If my son had died in a car crash or got hit by a bullet, I could bury him," she told one journalist. "I could say good-bye. But my son is in Syria. What can I do?"

I think of Ozana and the other mothers and fathers often. I will be bound with them in a strange fraternity for the rest of our lives. We were touched by the same horror. I wish them peace, but I'm not so sure many will find it.

I have another vision of life today. Before Jay disappeared, I was focused on earning money, going on vacations, getting ahead in the world. That's no longer the truth.

Despite the sadness and the anguish, the odyssey to save my

son made me a better person. I mean that sincerely. The disaster of Jay's disappearance gave me a chance to see other worlds and to expand my view of what's possible.

I took a huge risk in going to Syria and I succeeded. That has made me more confident in my abilities to navigate even hostile places. And the fact that a father's love prevailed, despite the savagery of the places I saw, gives me hope for the world around me. Syria is an open wound, but I know its people and I believe it will come back. One day, the terror of Islamic extremism will end.

But that day is still far off. We need to protect our children from the threats of recruitment and radicalization. Some people don't like to hear that; they believe that everything will work out in the end if we just ignore the dangers. What I would say to the people is: I was once like you. I didn't think action was necessary. I didn't think radicalization could happen in my own backyard. But it did. And it will spread far and wide if we don't stop it.

I discovered my philosophy of life in Syria: Find what you believe in and pursue it until the end of your strength. Always believe that you will win out in the end. If your dream is built on love, it can't lose. It may falter many times, but if you carry it forward, it will prevail. But you have to carry if forward; you have to act.

In one word: believe.

Acknowledgments

I would like to thank everyone—in Syria, Belgium, and elsewhere—who helped me in the search for my son. Without your dedication and courage, his rescue wouldn't have been possible. My sincere thanks to Kris Luyckx, who served as my son's lawyer and supplied hope when it was most needed. And special thanks to Donald Trump, whose book *Think Like a Champion* served as an inspiration throughout my ordeal.